FOLKLORE AND LEGENDS OF DARTMOOR

By WILLIAM CROSSING

With an Introduction by Brian Le Messurier

FOREST PUBLISHING

First published in 1997 by FOREST PUBLISHING, Woodstock, Liverton, Newton Abbot, Devon TQ12 6JJ

Copyright   © Forest Publishing 1997
              © Introduction Brian Le Messurier 1997

British Library Cataloguing in Publication Data

A catalogue record for this book is available from the British Library.

ISBN 0–9527297–5–X

Forest Publishing

Editorial, design and layout by:
Mike & Karen Lang

Typeset by:
Carnaby Typesetting, Torquay, Devon TQ1 1EG

Printed and bound in Great Britain by:
BPC Wheatons Ltd., Exeter, Devon EX2 8RP

Front cover illustration:

Lady Mary Howard travelling in her coach of bones drawn by headless horses.
(John W. Taylor)

CONTENTS

ACKNOWLEDGEMENTS

The Publishers wish to sincerely thank all of those people who have provided assistance during the compilation of this book. Particular thanks are due to Mr David Sullivan ('Dartmoor Dave') for drawing our attention to this series of articles; to Mr Brian Le Messurier for writing the Introduction; to Miss Elisabeth Stanbrook for allowing us to reproduce her photograph of Erme Pound; to the staff of the British Library (Newspaper Library) for providing photocopies of the original series of articles that appeared in *The Western Weekly Mercury Illustrated*.

LIST OF ILLUSTRATIONS

Publisher's Note:–

The above listed illustrations are the modern-day equivalents of all those that accompanied the original series of articles – little has changed!

INTRODUCTION

The discovery of this long-forgotten series of articles is probably the most exciting event for devotees of William Crossing (and everyone interested in Dartmoor literature) since the publication of 'Present Day Life on Dartmoor' as *Crossing's Dartmoor Worker* in 1966. That Crossing had written 'Folklore and Legends of Dartmoor' as late as 1914 was quite forgotten, and this series was not identified in *The Dartmoor Bibliography* (compiled by Peter Hamilton-Leggett, Devon Books, 1992) and *Supplements,* or noted in the list of his writings contained in the article by T. Cann Hughes printed in *The Devonian Year Book* in 1929, the year after his death.

Crossing had been incredibly active in the field of quasi-journalism in the 1890s and in the early years of this century, but his circumstances then changed. A brief account of his life is necessary to put the present book in context …

William Crossing was born in Plymouth on 14 November 1847 and spent much of his boyhood in that city. As a child he was encouraged by his mother to interest himself in the antiquities and traditions of the countryside, and since the family spent holidays in a cottage on Roborough Down he was introduced to Dartmoor at an early age.

When he left school he was apprenticed to a sail-cloth manufacturer, but, disliking the trade, ran away to sea and sailed to Canada. By the time he was twenty he had returned to Plymouth and was working for his father. In his spare time he wrote poetry and plays, and also took every opportunity to visit the moor which remained his chief interest.

Mr Crossing senior, no doubt feeling that a position of responsibility would benefit his son, sent William to supervise the family mill at South Brent. But away from parental control William indulged in his twin delights of drama and Dartmoor more freely than ever; he ran a local theatre, which after an initial success failed financially, and the moor was at his doorstep.

Theatricals continued to attract, and so William formed his own professional drama group with which he went on tour. When this venture failed, too, he returned to the South Brent mill, which his long-suffering father had kept going, and resumed his Dartmoor explorations. Perhaps because of his lack of interest it was not long before the canvas mill closed down, and he was left struggling for his livelihood. It is worth remembering, however, that with the development of steam propulsion at sea the need for ships' sails would have diminished.

He had married in 1872 and shortly afterwards began to keep careful records of his Dartmoor excursions and studies. With no desire to return to business he determined to earn his daily bread by writing, but he and his wife, Emma, stayed on at South Brent until the 1890s, when they moved to Brent Tor, and then to Mary Tavy. Until his health began to decline, Crossing had constantly walked or ridden the moor, never shirking a soaking in his tweed clothes and leather gaiters. Wherever he went he made friends with the moormen, and he was a popular figure in the group round the peat fire in the evenings, when he would play tunes on his tin whistle, or recite an improvised rhyme describing his wanderings of the day.

Crossing had joined the Dartmoor Preservation Association soon after it was formed in 1883, and was a member of the Devonshire Association from 1881 to 1891, although he never contributed to the *Transactions* of that body. From being a person of some substance – he writes in *Amid Devonia's Alps* of having 'a man' called George in 1872 – he became so impoverished that he had to resign from both Associations.

Much of Crossing's writing up to the early 1890s had been for a journal called *The Western Antiquary* which ran from 1881 to 1895. Contributors to this publication were not paid. Up to this time only *Amid Devonia's Alps* of Crossing's books had not first had an airing in the pages of *The Western Antiquary*.

In 1891 he wrote a long article called 'The Land of Stream and Tor' for *Doidge's Western Counties Illustrated Annual* for 1892. One feels it was prepared with a view to separate and simultaneous publication as a small book about Dartmoor, for it appeared under its own covers as *The Land of Stream and Tor* at about the same time. This little book was reprinted by Forest Publishing with an Introduction by the present writer in 1994.

By 1893 one senses he was finding it difficult to make ends meet.

From now until the end of the century he found such literary employment as he could, but this was a relatively barren period of his life. His health had deteriorated, and he was compelled to remain at home for long spells. He became editor of *The Westcountry Annual*, brought out a small book called *Cricket Averages* and other unexpected titles like *Mount Edgecumbe Souvenir, The Book of Fair Devon* and *The Marine and River Guide to the South Coast of Devon and Cornwall.*

William Crossing as he was in about 1895. The drawing is a copy of a photograph in *West-Country Poets*, 1896, and first appeared in *The Western Morning News* in 1904.

With the end of the nineteenth century he saw his opportunity to write a series of articles telling the story of the hundred years just past in so far as they affected Dartmoor. Thus 'A Hundred Years on

Dartmoor' began its seventeen-week run in *The Western Morning News* in June 1900. These articles were published a year later in book form with the addition of photographs and several appendices. The book was highly successful and went into five editions.

Arising from the success of *A Hundred Years ...*, Crossing was engaged to write 'Echoes of an Ancient Forest', and this series of thirteen articles began in *The Western Morning News* in November 1901. Reading between the lines, one suspects that 'Echoes ...' was commissioned with the intention of later publishing the articles as a book, but this didn't happen – until 1994, when Forest Publishing brought it out, once again with a scene-setting Introduction by the present writer.

Between 1901 and 1906 six further series of articles appeared in various West Country newspapers, and *The Dartmoor Bibliography* gives details of these. All have now been published in book form. He also contributed a chatty weekly column called 'Westcountry People and Places' in *The Western Weekly News* (now no longer in existence) from 1902 to 1909, but this was concerned with topics throughout the region, and included much verse and stories. It was probably his main regular source of income at that time, though in 1906 he became tutor to the three sons of Mr W.P. Collins, and teaching was carried on alongside work on his magnum opus, the *Guide to Dartmoor*. This went into three editions, in 1909, 1912 and 1914; the third edition, when it appeared in five separate parts, had a Preface variously dated April to July 1914, and inscribed "Black Down, Dartmoor", so we know where Crossing was living when he wrote this series of articles.

A rhyming letter from Crossing to Mr Collins has survived from 1910, which proves Crossing's facility as a versifier, and underlines the difficulty of travel in those days. Presumably Mr Collins had invited the Crossings to Throwleigh where he happened to be staying:-

Black Down
12 Aug 1910

Dear Mr Collins
Cheerless broke the day,
And showed us we at home would have to stay.
As we looked out upon the dismal scene
Nought met our gaze – no patch of blue nor green.
The clouds it seemed the distant hilltops kissed,
We couldn't see them though, since all was mist.

We waited – though not patiently – and then
Seeing the clock showed 'twas the hour of ten
And still 'twas dreary, what was I to do,
But send a telegram, informing you
That we at home would be obliged to stay,
And come to Throwleigh on another day.
Shall it be Monday? Well at any rate
'Tis then we'll come, and for you we will wait
Up at the station, 'bove Okehampton town,
And when you come will motor with you down.
Time – half-past twelve, as on the tables seen,
On Monday, August, day of month fifteen.
And then at Throwleigh, after all this tossing
Will rest, and take it easy,

William Crossing

Dartmoor and the West Country may have been his main interests, but the theatre continued to attract, and he collaborated with Florence Eaton to write a play called *The Triumph* which described man's conquest of tuberculosis. It was given a matinée performance on 27 November 1912 at the Royal Court Theatre before an audience which included King George V and Queen Mary.

It was in these years, too, that he was in demand as a lecturer in the towns and villages around Dartmoor. I have seen an undated reference to a talk he gave in Okehampton, and Wallace Perryman, who died in 1974 aged 88, once told me that as a young man he attended a summer lecture in Chagford School by Crossing and the room was full. In addition, as car ownership increased, he found employment as an official guide registered with the RAC to conduct visitors round the moorland roads in their own vehicles. Indeed, he even produced a little brochure entitled *Crossing Dartmoor* indicating as much on the front cover and bearing the address Mary Tavy, Devon, as well as a drawing of a car, *circa* 1914.

This brings us neatly to the year of publication of the articles which form this book. They appeared in *The Western Weekly Mercury Illustrated* beginning on 4 July 1914, and thus straddled the outbreak of what became known as the Great War.

No hint of this appalling conflict enters the articles which continued regularly until 17 October 1914. Crossing was now 67 and childless, but one of the Collins boys was to lose his life in the next four years: the other two, Jack and Ronald, lived on until recent times.

The newspaper headed each article with the words A FASCINATING SERIES BY WILLIAM CROSSING, and in smaller letters the first was prefaced by the introductory sentence 'Mr Crossing is the greatest living authority on the antiquities, folklore and legends of Dartmoor. Written in a popular style, the series of articles we begin today should prove among the most interesting yet published.'

Every article except one was illustrated with a photograph, though who took them is not stated. In the event, they could not be reproduced for this book, but the subjects have been re-photographed. Curiously, the illustration for Chapter 15 was of Dean Prior church, not Holne church as stated in the caption. Holne church appears in this book.

The material used by Crossing for this series of sixteen articles ranged over the gamut of Dartmoor folklore and legends. His other publications which touch on this topic, *Tales of the Dartmoor Pixies* and *Folk Rhymes of Devon,* can be seen from their titles to have a different emphasis. He enlivens his accounts with conversation between Dartmoor characters, and I leave it to readers to decide if his written attempt to convey the local dialect has succeeded. I have found that reading those parts of the book where dialogue is used are best read aloud.

Sadly, there are few biographical details to grab hold of, but we learn the names of his dogs and horses, and he informs us – perhaps with tongue in cheek – that he saw his only pixy as a boy of seven.

Crossing was never given to self-pity, and he conveys nothing of his reduced circumstances or health problems in these pages. The impact of 'acetylene lamps and hooters' is suggested as the failure of Lady Howard's coach to be seen in recent years! This somewhat cynical and down to earth sense of humour frequently surfaces as he describes a tradition you know he really has no time for. He often ends a chapter in this way, leaving a thought to hang in the air, as it were, until next week, for these articles originally came out weekly.

One last thing should be pointed out. In two places Crossing includes a recent event which I have not found mentioned elsewhere in his writings. In his chapter 'Old People and Old Places' he writes of Teign Head Farm how 'quite recently the old thatched roof has been replaced by one of slate.' While this was being done some putty had gone missing, and it was found inside one of the local sheep dogs!

The other 'new' story concerns what we now know as the Keble Martin Chapel beside the Wella Brook, below Huntingdon Warren House. This open-to-the-sky place of worship was established in 1909 by the Martin brothers. Many years later one of them, Keble Martin, became the best-selling author/illustrator of *The Concise British Flora*. (See the article by Audrey Harbord in *The Countryman* for Autumn 1973, reprinted in *The Countryman* for Spring 1994.)

We don't know if it was ever suggested that 'Folklore and Legends of Dartmoor' should be granted the permanence of a book. The outbreak of war may have modified any such plans. At all events, the series was overlooked and forgotten until now. One wonders if there are any other Crossing gems awaiting discovery!

Crossing's last years are touched with sadness. Mr Collins arranged a public subscription for him on his 70th birthday, but shortly afterwards the old couple had to move to Ivybridge, where relations lived, for Mrs Crossing was ailing. When constant nursing became necessary she was admitted to Tavistock Institution (the workhouse in common parlance), and she died there on 6 June 1921.

Mr Collins found accommodation for his old friend at Mary Tavy, and Crossing lived there for a while. In 1924, while he was away from home, the woman who looked after his rooms found a mass of papers and, because mice had damaged them, burnt the lot. Since Crossing had been preparing a history of Dartmoor, and the notes represented a lifetime's work, the loss was irreplaceable. For twelve weeks from 9 July 1925 he was a patient at Tavistock Institution, but in October he was taken to Cross Park Nursing Home, in Plymouth, where he spent his last three years. During this time Mr Collins paid the bills, which amounted to several hundred pounds. While at Cross Park he published his last book, a volume of poems called *Cranmere*, after the principal work it contained. His first book, *Leaves from Sherwood* (1868) was also poetry.

William Crossing died on 3 September 1928, and is buried with his wife in Mary Tavy churchyard. The grave is north-east of the church, and standing by it one can see the western slopes of Dartmoor swelling up less than a mile away.

Our debt to Crossing is enormous. He was the pioneer of a rational study of Dartmoor. He discovered stone crosses whose whereabouts had long been forgotten, and recorded their position in his books on the subject. He was the accurate chronicler of customs now gone from the country calendar, and his collection of folklore tales was made before the memory of them was lost forever. He gained the confidence and respect of Dartmoor people and from them learned the obscure place-names, and as a result of frequent forays across the whole of the moor at all times of the year acquired a minute knowledge of every hill and valley, and many of the antiquities which had been the subject of unproven theorising. He can be relied upon to present the true Dartmoor, unadorned by flights of fancy. It is good that a wider public can read his words once more, for although written so long ago, they have stood the test of time.

Brian Le Messurier
August 1997

❅❅❅❅❅

1

To and Fro in the Earth

The customs and superstitions of a people are always interesting as showing us the thoughts of men in primitive times. What are now but tales of wonder, stories of fairyland, were once beliefs seriously entertained by all. Such traditionary stories and legends belong to every land, and by comparing them we are often led to the discovery of their origin, and are enabled to see the meaning of much that would otherwise be obscure. It has been found that their source was often of a religious character, and that various customs looked upon by those who observed them as mere amusements had their root in ceremonies of much import. The charms of the country people are recognised as a survival of ancient magic, and certain practices current among them as being derived from an early form of worship.

That these stories continued to be believed long after the worship of mythical gods had been forgotten need not surprise us. An untutored people is always ready to accept as true that which is wonderful. And that such beliefs were fostered we have only to look into the monkish historians, and the accounts given us of saints, to be well assured of. When we find it gravely stated by those supposed to be teachers of men that wonderful miracles were wrought by saints, often merely to serve some selfish purpose, we can understand how other stories that had been handed down from father to son should continue to be believed. It was easy for a man to accept the statement that Jack the Giant Killer possessed a coat that would render him invisible when his spiritual leader told him that St. Goar had on one occasion hung his cape upon a sunbeam; or that the piety of St. Fechin was so fervent that it caused the cold water in which he washed to rise nearly to the boiling point. Such teaching would tend to strengthen old beliefs; in fact the examples of the wonders performed by the saints were founded in some degree on the myths of the people, and so we find that many of their superstitions had a long continuance, some of them existing even in our own day.

In a region like Dartmoor, which till a comparatively recent period was little intruded upon by the outside world, and in other remote districts, these archaic beliefs would find a place after faith in them had begun to weaken in the more populous centres. It is true that except in the matter of charms and, as it is termed, ill-wishing, the country people no longer place credence in the stories related by their grandsires, but not a few of them may still be heard nevertheless. I have listened to many a story of the moor as I have sat near the hearth before the glowing peat, but I do not remember that anything very wonderful had come within the personal experience of the narrators themselves. Such were usually accounts of what had befallen others, and were more often than not something of which those relating the adventure had only 'heerd tell'. Among those whose quaint stories never failed to interest me I may name my old friend, Richard Cleave, of Hexworthy, Will Mann, of the same place, Uncle George Caunter, of Dartmeet, John Bishop, of Swincombe, and Richard Eden, who in his early days lived at Fox Tor. I have also recollections of Willcocks, of Roborough Down, of Shillibeer, of Sheepstor, and, in a nearer day, of Elias Leaman, of Widecombe, and John Burn and Uncle Jimmy Stephens, of Mary Tavy. Of these not one remains. They sleep in quiet churchyards on the fringe of the moor, but their memory is yet green.

As in the folk tales of other lands, we meet with the good and the bad in our Dartmoor traditions. The Arch Enemy of mankind figures in not a few of them, and if I commence with noticing some of these it must not be supposed that I do so because I regard him as being entitled to our first consideration, but simply for the reason that no account of Dartmoor folklore would be complete without some notice of his doings. Being, therefore, compelled, as it were, to give these some attention, it seems more convenient to do so at once in order that we may get him out of the way.

The deeds of Satan while "going to and fro in the earth," and "walking up and down in it," invariably reveal him in conflict with man, though he is usually very careful to hide his real intentions and let it appear as though he desired to help him. Whether this was the case when he once encountered a powerful adversary on the hills above the deep gorge of the Teign we have been unable to discover, for the story merely tells us of the conflict, and says nothing about what led to it. His antagonist, no less a personage than the redoubtable King Arthur, seems to have given him as good as he sent, for when Satan, mounting a lofty height, commenced to fling quoits at the British king, he speedily found himself assailed in a similar manner. Arthur took his stand on another hill about a mile distant, and from its summit discharged his missiles with terrific effect. As the quoits fell they became changed into masses of rock, and these may still be seen. Their number is considerable, and we may therefore conclude not only that the engagement lasted some time, but also that it was of a desperate character. But eventually Satan found that he had met with his match and was glad to beat a retreat, leaving Arthur triumphant. The hill on which the king took his stand is situated near the road leading from Moretonhampstead to Bridford, and is known as Blackystone. The enemy had entrenched himself on Hel Tor, further to the north. This name simply implies height, and is found, often as a compound, in many places.

Now this story is not a mere invention suggested by certain circumstances. It had its formation in men's belief. Long before the period in which King Arthur is supposed to have lived the opposing powers of good and evil were recognised, and fables concerning conflicts between these had originated. This Dartmoor story is only a later variant of one of these fables, applied to the locality in which we find it in order to account for the scattered masses of granite to be seen there. Satan stands for all that is evil; King Arthur the brave and true, for all that is good.

The spirit of the British king is still abroad; it would be ill with mankind were it otherwise. Tradition tells us that it inhabits the body of a chough, a kind of jackdaw, which frequents rocky places and is found on the Cornish coast. Hence it is impious to raise the hand against one of those birds lest it might prove the earthly habitation of the spirit of the valiant Arthur. That it has flown over Dartmoor there is, happily, abundant proof. One spot perpetuates its name. Near the springs of the West Webburn is a hollow that is still known as Chough Gully.

In the cases of Blackystone and Hel Tor the conflict led to the formation of those rock masses, but in other instances we find that Satan has wrought the partial destruction of tors. One side of Brent Hill is covered with granite blocks, dislodged by the touch of time. Story credits Satan with the work, though what his object was is not stated. Possibly he did it when nothing better presented itself, being desirous of practically illustrating the truth of the lines that he is never at a loss to find mischief for idle hands to do. Rocks and boulders encumber many of the hillsides of Dartmoor, and the channels of its rivers. The true explanation of this did not satisfy men in an earlier day. They attributed their presence to supernatural agency, and hence old stories tell us that Satan flung them there. We may instance the valley of the Plym above Shaugh Bridge. Here the rocks were cast down from the Dewer Stone Hill during a storm the Enemy raised to vent his rage for some fancied wrong — possibly the missing of a hoped-for prey. He has also been known to raise mighty floods and to turn the crystal streams of the moor into raging torrents. One Sunday afternoon in the year 1628, when the people of Okehampton came from church, they were surprised to find that the eastern branch of the Ockment, which runs through the town, had risen to a great height, and was flowing with an impetuosity such as they had never before known. There was no sign of rain, and the western branch of the river presented its usual appearance. It was very strange, and nobody was able to offer an explanation of the circumstance. But presently curiosity was set at rest. An examination was made of the water, and the murder was out. In the words of the old Okehampton chronicler, John Rattenbury, "the water did savour and smell of some brimstone". This was proof conclusive. While the good folks had been at their devotions, Satan had been busy on the moor.

His work is found everywhere, but on Dartmoor he certainly seems to have devoted his attention to high places. His footprints may be seen on many of the tors, and since these are pressed deeply into the solid rock it is evident his tread was not of the lightest. It was on an elevated spot that he prepared his food. On Mis Tor his frying-pan may yet be seen, a large utensil, measuring a yard in diameter and of proportionate depth. There are conflicting reports of what he usually cooked in it, some hinting that those who dwelt in the vicinity of the rocks often smelt something proceeding from the pile of the same nature as that with which the river at Okehampton was suspected of being impregnated. But a certain moorman once gave a different account. He happened to be passing over the moor, and on drawing near the tor suddenly became aware that the air was laden with a powerful odour. The meaning of it flashed upon his mind in an instant, and digging his heels into his pony's sides he set off down the hill at a gallop. Arriving at Merrivale, he told his story, and when asked what the smell resembled, said it put him in mind of nothing so much as the frying of 'risty-bacon'.

It is not everybody who is honoured by having a tor on Dartmoor called after him. But Satan is; unless you choose to put it the other way and say it is not every tor on Dartmoor that is dishonoured by bearing his name. Devil's Tor near the head of the Cowsic is his lasting monument, though why that particular mass should have been fixed upon to keep his memory alive I have never been able to discover. It is by no means a striking memorial, and would hardly satisfy some people. It has, indeed, been thought that the menhir known as Bear Down Man, which stands near by, is the real monument, and that the tor simply takes its name from that fact. But were the latter of the most imposing appearance it would serve its supposed purpose no better, for one with such a notoriety as Satan possesses requires no memorial at all.

It is not to be supposed that Satan is fond of church-going, but he visits them sometimes. In a church in Cornwall a small door used formerly to be opened during baptisms in order that when renounced the fiend might readily take his departure. This was called the Devil's door, and was in the north side of the church. That is the quarter favoured by evil spirits, and thus everything was made as convenient as possible for him. His presence in these sacred edifices is usually due to a desire to work mischief, and so rooted is his antipathy to them that he has been known to endeavour to prevent the building of them. The churches of Brent Tor, Buckfastleigh, and Plympton furnish instances of this. The first-named was intended to be built at the foot of the lofty peak which it now crowns. But the builders had not proceeded far with their work when they were surprised on arriving at the scene of their labours one morning to find that the stones they had already placed in position had been removed. A diligent search was made for them, and at length they were discovered on the summit of the hill. They were brought down, and the work of building recommenced. When the men ceased their labour parts of the walls had again risen a foot or two above the ground, and though hardly supposing that they would be thrown down again, it was not with an entire absence of misgiving that they went to their homes. That night, when those who possessed clocks and happened to be awake, heard them strike the hour of twelve, a tall, dark figure approached the site of the intended church. With a contemptuous gesture he raised his foot, and with a few powerful kicks levelled the work of the builders. Then, with equal expedition, he conveyed the stones to the top of the conical hill which he had determined should be the site of the church. His power was not sufficient to enable him to stop the building of it altogether, but he had some control over the work, and was determined that if there was to be a church it should be placed in a situation difficult of access, by which he hoped that very few would ever attend it.

Once more the workmen arrived on the spot where they had laid their foundations, but not a stone was to be seen. They guessed now where they should find them, and it was not long before they were brought from the tor a second time. But they might have spared themselves the trouble of removing them, for their indefatigable foe that night again conveyed them to the summit of the crag that crested the hill. This was several times repeated, and then it became plain to the labourers that Satan had set himself against them. As they recognised that they were no match for the Devil, it was decided that they must let him have his way, and so it was agreed that they should erect the church on the tor.

A similar story is told regarding the building of Buckfastleigh Church, which stands on a hill near the town, but in this case the builders, after allowing the Evil One to have his own way, formed a long flight of steps from the lower ground to the church, which, if not rendering it altogether so easy of access as might be desired, at least thwarted Satan's design. It is said that you seldom find a rogue without finding a fool, and whether this be generally true or not, it is certain that in the matter of choosing sites for churches Satan did not show himself very clever. In seeking to render them inconvenient of approach in order to deter worshippers from attending them, he usually compelled their builders to place them in situations where they could not fail to be seen, and thus drew many to them, that without such a reminder of their existence might have got into the habit of staying away.

But it is difficult to fathom the intentions of this malignant spirit who is "walking up and down" in the earth. He is said to have been connected with the building of the church of Plympton St. Mary, but in this instance he acted in a manner quite the reverse of those just cited. It was decided to erect a church on the high ground known as Crownhay Castle, and work was commenced. For a few days all went well, but on the builders coming to their work one morning they were amazed at finding that all traces of their walls had vanished. That this was the work of the Evil One they all agreed; but what had become of the stones? They searched everywhere, but their quest was fruitless. At length news was brought that the missing masonry was to be seen on the shore of the creek which in early times extended upward from the Laira nearly to the town. The master builder, nothing daunted, at once ordered its removal to the intended site on Crownhay, and work was once more commenced there. But the Devil was not to be thwarted. He again removed the stones to the waterside in the hope that some exceptionally high tide would sweep the church away. As he continued to do this as often as they were brought back, the builders deemed it politic to concede the point to him, and started to erect their edifice on the spot on which their powerful antagonist insisted. But the men of Plympton were as wise as the 'old serpent'. When their church was finished they protected it from the waters of the creek by a strong wall, and Satan found that he was beaten after all.

It is obvious that these stories sprang up among the people when it was desired to account for the erection of certain churches in inconvenient situations. But, as before observed, they were not entire inventions. At some early time the walls of a church in course of building had perhaps been overthrown during a tempest, and many of the stones carried to a distance by floods. As it was not to be supposed that the Ruler of all things would permit a building intended for religious purposes to be demolished, the destructive work was attributed to Satan. He it was who had raised the storm; and by-and-by, when the story came to be told without mentioning the latter, the Devil was credited with having kicked down the building and carrying off the stones. All this was, of course, very unfair. It was a case of giving a dog a bad name when he did not deserve it, and constrains us, who live in a more enlightened age, to admit the truth of the saying that the Devil is not so black as he is painted.

Sometimes Satan has been charged with having raised a storm in order to bring about the destruction of a church, presumably for the reason that the work being accomplished there interfered with his own. But there are no stories showing that he has succeeded in destroying any churches in the parishes bordering upon Dartmoor, which are the only ones now under consideration. But there is more than one tale that tells of great damage having been wrought, and among these the story of the Widecombe storm of 1638 is not the least wonderful. But if moorland tradition be correct this does not appear to have been brought about for the reason above suggested. Satan's visit to the church, and the dreadful storm it occasioned, was for the purpose of claiming as his own one who had bartered his soul for a brief period of worldly enjoyment.

In my youthful days more than one story used to be told of the 'wicked Jan Reynolds', of Widecombe, and of the sad end to which he came. Having entered into a compact with Satan whereby he was to be provided with what money he needed until such time as he should be found in Widecombe Church, when he was to become Satan's prey, he set about 'enjoying himself', which meant indulging in every sort of wickedness. Jan thought himself secure, for the church was the last place he desired to go. One version of the story has it that Jan was to be discovered asleep in the church; but, however that may be, the day fell when his ghostly enemy became aware that Jan, forgetting himself or being muddled with drink, was at the afternoon service at Widecombe. Mounting his black steed, Satan set out at a gallop for the village, stopping for a brief space at the inn at Pound's Gate in order to refresh

Interior view of the church of Widecombe-in-the-Moor.

himself and inquire the way. Arriving at the church, he flung himself from his horse and darted towards the porch. Immediately a thick darkness fell, and as he entered the building one of the pinnacles of the tower, struck by lightning, fell bodily on to the roof of the nave, and a terrific peal of thunder awoke the echoes of the valley. Satan strode to the seat in which Jan Reynolds had ensconced himself and seized him by the neck. Then it became apparent what the wretched youth had been engaged in. In his hand were four cards, but though they were aces they were to bring him no more luck. The Devil vaulted into the saddle, and giving his steed the rein the animal mounted into the air and disappeared in the gloom. The cards fell from Jan Reynolds's hand, and ere they reached the ground became transformed into small newtakes. These enclosures may still be seen on the side of the hill near where the West Webburn rises; they bear a rude resemblance in form to the pips on the cards.

It is not always that we hear of Satan bearing off his victims to the accompaniment of thunder and lightning. Sometimes he spirits them away quietly. This may, or may not, have been the case with the peasant who mysteriously disappeared from Foale's Arrishes under Rippon Tor, or with the man who, crossing Sheeps Tor Bridge late one night, was never after seen in the parish. Time was when much that appeared wonderful was put down to Satan, but we think in the above cases the verdict should be of 'not proven'. This must be our verdict, too, in the charge that has been brought against him of having once kept alive a feud that existed between the men of Tavistock and those of Okehampton. It has been stated that he watched the progress of this from the lofty standpoint of Amicombe. We will frankly own that we do not believe it.

Joy spread over Dartmoor one day. It was reported that the Devil was no more; that he had died of cold at North Lew. A farmer had pulled his carcase out of the mire, horns and tail complete, all plentifully bedaubed with black mud. But the joy was short-lived when it was discovered that the supposed materialised demon was nothing more than a stag — an animal which the farmer had never before seen — which had perished in the bog.

But may not the farmer have been right after all? It would seem so, for I will vouch for it that the Devil has never since that time been seen on Dartmoor.

❋❋❋❋❋

2

Giants and Strong Men

Dimmed by the years, and as elusive as the Will-o'-the-wisp, certain stories, or fragments of stories, are found in various parts of Dartmoor that show us that there was a time when people believed that this wild hill country had its Rephaim and its sons of Anak. Little that is connected can be gathered, and that little is fast disappearing. But less than a hundred years ago the Dartmoor folk well remembered how their elders used to speak of the giants that formerly held possession of the moor. It was at a time, they said, when the tors shot up from the midst of great forests, a statement which we shall not be the least inclined to doubt. To this race of men they attributed the erection of the stone monuments of the moor — the dolmen, the columnar circle, and the menhir. This was their belief, and as those who erected them were men of huge size and great strength, they saw nothing very wonderful in the accomplishment of work that would have presented almost insuperable difficulties to men of ordinary size. It was an easy way of accounting for that which they did not understand. Stories connecting the giants with ancient stone monuments are found in other parts. We know that in the twelfth century Stonehenge was called the Giants' Dance.

The first that we hear of giants in connection with the hill country of the West is in the legend of Tamara, which is noticed in the chapter on the lore of the Dartmoor streams. But it tells us nothing about them; we merely learn that the beautiful maiden who was transformed into the river Tamar was a daughter of that mighty race; of story concerning them there is none. But in later times, though yet removed from us by nearly eight centuries, something more definite is told us; not in legend, but in Geoffrey of Monmouth's *History of Britain*. Unfortunately Geoffrey, notwithstanding he was Bishop of St. Asaph, is not to be relied upon; his writings will not bear the light of modern criticism, and we must therefore receive his statements with much caution. But what he tells us is nevertheless interesting, and probably this was the chief end he had in view when writing his marvellous account of our country. Speaking of Britain, he says: "The island was then called Albion, and was inhabited by none but a few giants", and then he goes on to tell us about some of those who belonged to the West-country. Among these was "one detestable monster named Goemagot, in stature twelve cubits, and of such prodigious strength that at one shake he pulled up an oak as if it had been a hazel wand". This formidable adversary having been defeated and captured in an encounter with the Britons, in which twenty of his companions were slain, was brought out to wrestle with Corineus, the brave commander who, according to the fable, accompanied Brutus, the Trojan, to these shores about the year 1200 B.C. Corineus proved victorious, for, lifting the giant on his shoulders, he ran with him to a high rock and hurled him into the sea. The scene of the encounter was the hill on which the Plymouth Citadel now stands, and Geoffrey states that the spot from which the giant was thrown was in his day known as Goemagot's Leap. Tristram Risdon, of Winscott, in North Devon, a very different kind of historian from Geoffrey, writing some 500 years after him, refers to these great men of a former age. In his account of Lydford he speaks of it as being exposed to the Dartmoor storms, and says it was more fitted for "the giant-like Albionists such as are reported to be the first inhabiters of this island", than for people of greater civilisation.

Goemagot was thrown from the rock where the Plym pours its waters into the sea, and it therefore seems not unfitting that we should find some traces of giants on that river. These are encountered before it has gone far upon its way. From its brink rises Giant's Hill, and near by is a cairn that bears the name of the Giant's Basin. Whether this part of Dartmoor in which the Plym has its source ever was the haunt of giants I cannot at present say, but I shall be quite prepared to affirm that it was so when I am satisfied that Corineus wrestled with Goemagot and beat him. When that is established it will be easy to prove that his brother giants prepared porridge in the basin on the Plym, and stirred it with the menhirs that are seen near by. We shall also be quite ready to show that what has been supposed to be the basements of circular-shaped huts are really petrified rings thrown there by the "first inhabiters of this island", who used them as quoits.

But there will always be doubting Thomases, no matter what proofs are brought forward, and I am fully aware that I should be unable to get all to see with me. But others there are who will be ready to believe that giants once inhabited Dartmoor, provided that certain matters were first rendered indisputable. For instance, let us make our way to the steep hill that forms one side of the romantic gorge through which the West Ockment forces its way towards the beautiful Island of Rocks. There we shall find a tor, a pile of grey granite, which is known as the Slipper Stones. The observer sees at once the reason why it bears such a name. The topmost rock presents a rude resemblance to a huge slipper, and local story tells us that such it once was. Now it is only for us to be satisfied of the truth of this report, and the question of the existence of giants on the moor is conclusively proved, for nobody but a giant could have required such a slipper. It is simply a question of demonstrating that two and two make five, which is easy enough if it can first be shown that two is equal to three when required to be so.

Let us pass along this lofty ridge that rises above the Ockment. There is much to delight us, and we shall feel amply rewarded for our pains, even though the traces of the giants be but slight. But if our faith in the matter of the slipper be not weak, we shall probably regard the evidence we find here as satisfactory. On the slope of Corn Ridge we come upon two rocks which together are known as Branscombe's Loaf and Cheese. Whatever the bishop of that name may have had to do with these objects, it is quite certain that if ever they were what their names would lead us to suppose, none but a giant, and that a very big one, could have required them. It will be well, perhaps, for the visitor not to allow his antiquarian instincts to impel him to make too strict an inquiry into the matter, or he may learn that the first word has nothing whatever to do with bread, but (without the a) is simply a Celtic word, meaning a lump or excrescence. We are not out for antiquarian discoveries. We are in quest of evidence concerning giants, and, having discovered it, let us be content.

On Mardon Down, near Moretonhampstead, is a despoiled tumulus called the Giant's Grave. We can learn little or nothing about the giant, but the name shows us that there was a time when this huge race was spoken of in the locality. At a little distance from the tumulus is a short pillar, sometimes referred to as the Maximajor Stone, and by some said to represent the giant's staff. If this giant approached in size the one who could sit down before such a loaf and cheese as are to be seen on Corn Ridge we should be much more inclined to believe that the pillar represented his toothpick.

The notion that men of extraordinary size once inhabited the country was, of course, a survival of a belief of great antiquity, and the occasional arising of an Og or a Goliath was probably regarded as confirmatory of the truth of the stories that had been handed down. Additional proof was no doubt supposed to be afforded by the discoveries of bones of extinct animals which were mistaken for those of men. A few ribs, or teeth, of the megatherium, for instance, would be sufficient to convince men of an earlier period that the world was once peopled by beings of gigantic proportions. Risdon speaks of "the skeleton of a huge body" that was to be seen in his day at Buckfastleigh. What is meant is not quite clear, but the skeleton was such, he says, "whereby may be conceived what bigness once it bore, whose ruins may move the beholders both to wonder and pity".

The giants were usually possessed of great strength, which, of course, is what one would naturally suppose. Among the feats performed by them, those of one have come down to us whose doings it is a pleasure to record. We refer to Ordulph, son of Ordgar, Earl of Devon, who in the tenth century founded Tavistock Abbey. That he was a good giant will be at once apparent when it is stated that it was his custom to rise in the night and go out of doors to say his prayers. Probably like the eugenists of the present day, he was fully alive to the beneficial properties of fresh air. Ordulph evidently thought that it was impossible to have too much of it, and desired to set a good example. This has been followed by the eugenists — we are referring to that part of his practice concerning fresh air — which affords a further proof of the truth of the saying that there is nothing new under the sun.

Probably no greater man ever visited Dartmoor than this giant who was given to nocturnal devotions, and it is also likely that no one was ever known who was so well fitted for rambling over it. Anyone who has walked a few miles over its hills will be aware that certain impediments are constantly encountered. Here a feather-bed, as it is termed — a depression in the granite filled with slush, and covered with inviting-looking bright green moss, and there a stream with no apparent means of crossing it. To Ordulph such presented no obstacles. We learn something about him from William of Malmesbury, who wrote in the twelfth century, and among other matters that this saintly giant was able to stride over a river ten feet wide. Such an accomplishment would enable a man to treat as very light matters the impediments he would meet with on Dartmoor. That he was very strong is evident from the fact of his breaking down the gates and part of the wall of Exeter, and it seems rather unfair that he should not have received the credit due to him for having performed such a feat. Some there were who fully appreciated this Samson-like act, and were loud in expressing their admiration of it, but the king, in whose presence it took place, gave it as his opinion that it must have been done by the power of Satan. Now if Ordulph had been a wicked man such a remark might not be deemed surprising, but to suppose that the Evil One would be likely to help a man who was in the habit of leaving his warm bed in the middle of the night and going out into the cold to pray is altogether absurd. It is only fair to state that it has been said that the king merely pretended to believe that Satan had a part in the matter, desiring to make light of the deed.

Several writers, besides William of Malmesbury, have left us something about Ordulph. Risdon calls him "that great Duke of Devonshire", and states that his coat-armour was formerly to be seen in Werrington Church, which was one of the possessions the duke gave to Tavistock Abbey. Browne Willis, in speaking of that abbey, says that when he wrote the sepulchural effigy of Ordulph, which he states was of great length, lay under an arch in the north side of the cloisters of the abbey church. The upper portion of this archway may still be seen in the graveyard at Tavistock: the lower portion is now beneath the level of the surrounding ground. The Rev. E. A. Bray, writing in the early part of the last century, states that it was then related that in excavating for some foundations on the site of the abbey the workmen discovered a large stone coffin containing bones. When Mr. Bray wrote, these bones were preserved in the church, and were called the giant's bones. They consisted of two thigh bones, one being twenty-one inches in length and the other nineteen and a half inches. As we can hardly suppose that Ordulph had one leg longer than the other it would seem that one of these bones belonged to somebody else. We believe that a former sexton used to show them as the bones of the Saxon giant and his wife. If he was right in this it proves that Ordulph possessed a good sense of proportion, and was desirous of showing that, while looking down upon everybody around him, he would at least choose for a consort one who was on a level with himself.

But, while we always find the giants possessed of great strength, we have also instances of strong men who were not giants. Of these perhaps the foremost was Ephraim of Widecombe-in-the-Moor. He was regarded by his associates as a 'fine strappin' fella', certainly, but was not bigger than many others in the locality. His prowess showed itself chiefly in wonderful leaps and feats of strength. While he could not stride, like Ordulph, across a ten-feet stream, he found no difficulty in jumping across one of much greater width; and if he could not batter down the gates of a city he was able, at all events, to unhang with one hand any field-gate in the neighbourhood, and carry a couple of them about with ease. If it was required to move a granite boulder, and no horse and sledge were available, Ephraim was always ready to undertake the task, being able to roll a huge boulder with as little effort as most men would use to trundle a cart-wheel. To the miller of Cockington he was often of the greatest service, for not only was he able to unload his sacks of corn with expedition, but when it was required to dress the mill-stones Ephraim could lift them in a trice, and so render the fixing of ropes and blocks unnecessary. It was wonderful to see how he could toss about a crowbar — or bar ire, as the Dartmoor peasant calls it. It appeared little more than a straw in his hands, and not a few there were who believed that he could have bent it easily had he chosen.

One day certain feats of strength happened to be the theme of conversation among a little knot of villagers who were gathered on Widecombe Green. One said he could do this, and another said he could do that, and all seemed to be very confident of their ability to accomplish various things that nobody else would venture to undertake. In the midst of their talk Ephraim chanced to approach, and immediately the conversation took a fresh turn, those who had before been boasting of their performances the most loudly now appearing the most anxious to say nothing about them. But Ephraim had overheard enough to acquaint him with the nature of their remarks, and, confident of his own powers, told them flatly that there was not one among them who could carry so heavy a weight as he could. There was a dead silence, for all were well aware that Ephraim was far more than their match. But this was at length broken by one who conceived the idea of getting out of the corner in which Ephraim had pinned them by challenging the strong man to do something that he deemed impossible. He offered to wager that Ephraim could not carry a sack of corn upon his back from Widecombe to Post Bridge, a distance of five miles, without putting it down and resting.

To carry a sack of corn five miles on a good level road would be a feat requiring much strength and endurance, but when the nature of the ground between the places named comes to be considered it appears to be a task that even the strongest man could not achieve. But Ephraim believed himself to be equal to it, and without any hesitation accepted the wager.

The first part of the way lay over the huge ridge of Hameldon, and it was desperate work to reach the summit. But this was accomplished in time, and Ephraim then had the descent of Gore Hill before him. This

Post Bridge, showing the old clapper bridge in the foreground.

was easy enough for a man of such wondrous powers and it was not long before he crossed the Blackaton Brook. Then another hill had to be climbed, which, though not presenting such difficulties as Hameldon, nevertheless proved sufficiently formidable. Ephraim passed slowly up, and then the spirits of those who had become his backers ran high. There was only one short hill to be ascended now, and then Ephraim would have a practically level run in. It was reached. It is only a pinch, said his backers; Ephraim will do it. But the strong man did not do it. He tried it, like the good, staunch fellow that he was, but it proved too much for him. He was compelled to cast the sack from his shoulders, and the spot has ever since been known by the name of Ephraim's Pinch.

Mr. Edward Coaker, formerly of Hexworthy, told me this story many years ago, but as a true Dartmoor man he was careful to point out that although Ephraim lost his bet, he nevertheless succeeded in accomplishing a feat of which any man might be proud.

Another moorland Samson, of whom I have heard old people speak, once lived in the parish of South Brent. His feats were somewhat similar to those related of Ephraim, and he also possessed wonderful agility. Having once been challenged to leap over the turnpike gate at Brent Bridge, which was a particularly high one, he not only proved himself equal to the task, but performed it with a reaping-hook in each hand.

✳✳✳✳✳

3

The Dragon and the Serpent

In the investigation of the rude stone monuments found in various parts of the country, and indeed throughout the world, numerous speculative theories have been advanced, and those on Dartmoor have not escaped becoming the subjects of these ingenious exercises. To the plain man the intention of some of them at least is evident, but the older antiquaries apparently were not satisfied with what seems a simple explanation. Among a certain class of remains on the moor are large, circular enclosures, the walls of which are now invariably seen in a ruinous condition, called by the moormen 'pounds'. The unbiassed observer, or one not seeking to discover some abstruse meaning in them, would see that such a term described them correctly. They were, of course, built for the purpose of sheltering something, and as the remains of huts which investigation has conclusively proved were once occupied by men are found much greater number outside than inside these enclosures, it becomes evident that they were not erected for their use entirely. They were, in fact, cattle pounds, but that huts were seen within them is only what might be expected, as it would be necessary that some of the people should be near at hand to keep guard over the herd, especially at certain times. We can well understand how indispensable these pounds would be. At a period when wild animals ranged over the moor the cattle would need to be protected at night. Of course, we may reasonably suppose that in the event of those who dwelt around them being attacked by an enemy they would, if the shelter of walls required, seek refuge within them, but that is a very different thing from imagining them to have been built with such an end in view. In that case some lofty and less easily accessible spot would certainly have been chosen, and such are to be found all over Dartmoor. But this explanation has not always satisfied the antiquary. Notwithstanding that, except in one or two instances, and those occurring on the edge of the moor, they are placed in situations which it is difficult to believe

Grim's Pound.

would have been chosen had defence against a foe been their primary object. Certain investigators have preferred to regard them as forts, presumably because the wall is constructed in much the same way as that of undoubted hill forts in other parts of the county. In another case where the wall is more massive, and the enclosure itself larger than is usually seen, the pound was imagined to be something of quite another character. It was nothing less than a temple of the sun.

Another class of monument consisting of a row of stones extending for some distance over the moor, and probably sepulchral in its character, has been the subject of nearly a dozen different suggestions, one of them being that the rows were parts of serpents' temples. Thus the idea was that the moor was once the scene of sun and serpent worship. That relics of this form of idolatry are found in different parts of the world is well known, and it is impossible to say that it did not once obtain on Dartmoor. All that we can affirm is that there is nothing to be found there to lead us to suppose that such was the case. It is quite true that in some parts of the world certain stone monuments bear evidence that they were connected with such worship, and banks of earth and rude alignments of stones are found which seem to have been intended as representations of the serpent. But there is nothing on Dartmoor that connects itself with solar and serpent worship, unless it is contended that stone circles represent the sun. The stone rows are all practically straight, and exhibit nothing of that winding form which we should expect to see had a representation of a serpent been intended.

It sometimes happens that where evidence of one kind is wanting testimony of another character is forthcoming, and what the stone monuments fail to show may, perhaps, be found in the lore of the people. But little reveals itself in this connection, and, it may be said, nothing that is peculiar to the moor, so that there appears to be very slight grounds for supposing that the worship of the sun and the serpent — one the emblem of that which was beneficent, the other the symbol of wickedness, and worshipped only in fear — was ever introduced into Dartmoor. But at the same time it may well be that the earliest men who penetrated into that region brought with them traditions of that worship, even if they did not practice it themselves. From these may have come the few fragmentary stories once current among the moor people of dragons and winged serpents that used to haunt the valleys.

Scattered over every part of Dartmoor, except on the fen, which consists almost entirely of peat, are various remains of the people who in a bygone day dwelt among these hills, the object most commonly met with being a small ring of stones ranging from about twelve feet or fourteen feet in diameter to about double that size. These, of course, are familiar objects to the moorman, who not being prone to indulge in antiquarian speculations, regards them as the ruins of little circular houses, erected in some far-off time. They are, in fact, the dwellings of which we have already spoken as being sometimes found within the pounds, but more often without such an enclosing wall, and are known to the antiquary as hut circles. It is not so long ago that the moor folk had a tradition concerning the time of the erection of these huts. They were built, they used to say, in the days when there were dragons on the moor. These monsters had retreats in the narrow valleys of the secluded parts of it, from which they would issue to attack men who chanced to descend from the heights around. Discoveries of bones, such as we have referred to as possibly having given rise to the stories of the former presence of giants, may have tended to keep alive those traditions. In a French work on fossils is a description of the skull of a cave bear, which the author considered was the skull of a dragon, and it has also been supposed that the roc, the huge bird by means of which, as readers of the *Arabian Nights* will remember, Sindbad escaped from the Valley of Diamonds, was suggested by the discovery of a fossil tichorhine rhinoceros.

Not far from the confluence of the West Dart and the Wo Brook may be seen part of a hut circle to which a gable end has been added, the latter evidently the work of the tinners of medieval times. I have heard it stated in the locality that this little building was erected by the 'old men' for the purpose of keeping their tools in, and that this was done in some far-off day when dragons haunted the Wo Brook valley. By the 'old men' the moor folk mean the tin-streamers, and do not connect them with the people who erected the rude monuments of the moor, so there is evidently some confusion here. An old tradition in which dragons were associated with the valley appears to have lingered in the locality, and the hut circle, being different in character from those usually seen, consequent upon the addition that has been made to it, was thought to have something to do with it, and so was brought into the story. The reference to the tools evidently had its rise in the fact that workmen were in the habit of concealing these when they left the scene of their labours, and it is, of course, quite possible that they did leave them in the hut in question. I have myself found cutting-irons hidden beneath surface turf near the peat-beds, and on several of the streams are little buildings covered with turf, evidently meant for places of concealment, and called in consequence caches. The latter, as their situation plainly shows, were used by the tinners. Possibly there was a time when a connected story was related regarding the Wo Brook and the monsters which made their retreat in the hollow through which it runs. We possess only a remnant of it, but it is sufficient to throw some light on what would otherwise be entirely hidden.

I remember once hearing Richard Eden, one-time moorman in the south quarter, relate how not long before he had seen a number of snakes gathered in a small, shallow pit near Ringleshutts Gert on Holne Moor. They were clustered round its side, and some were coiled up in the bottom of it. Nobody ventured an opinion as to the meaning of it, but it was plain that it was thought that something mysterious was attached to the circumstance. But the tradition that in all probability once obtained on the moor had long been forgotten. In an earlier day men would have looked for such a thing at a certain time, for it was once believed that on Midsummer Eve it was usual for snakes to assemble and to form the egg, or serpent's stone, to an accompaniment of hisses. The finder of this wonderful object was a fortunate man, for its possessor would be sure to meet with success in all his undertakings. I did not go to the pit to look for the magic egg which, perhaps, is to be deplored. It is said that snakes do meet in companies, so that Eden's experience would not appear to be unique.

A writer who has now passed away, has said that the Dartmoor man is afraid of snakes. I will go farther and say that he is afraid of nothing. We must agree to allow some license to a novelist, but it is hardly fair to make assertions affecting men's courage when there is no ground whatever for doing so. The Dartmoor man has no greater dread of snakes than other men have, probably not so much, for familiarity with them breeds contempt. But he is not fond of them either, and certainly the days of serpent worship are gone by on the moor. And of the sun, too, for that matter, though it is appreciated a good deal more than the other. True, the Dartmoor native remembers when drinking in company to pass the cup 'round with the sun', but in doing this he is worshipping Bacchus rather than Sol. And it is not so very long ago that he might have sought Bel Tor, above the gorge of the Dart, in order to see the reflection of the rising sun in the water collected in the rock basin in its moving stones, and thus ensure good fortune; or he might even have visited the well in Okehampton Park for very much the same purpose; but in either case he would be unaware that what he did had ever any religious signification.

In the valley of the West Dart, above Two Bridges, is the well-known Wistman's Wood, where stunted oaks grow from the midst of a clatter, or congeries of granite masses. This the imagination of antiquaries has connected with the Druids, and since those ancient priests are said to have invested the serpent with a mysterious character it seems only fitting that the wood should be connected with snakes also. The only reasons for supposing that the Druids were ever seen there are that the oak grows there, and that the name of the wood may possibly be a corruption of the words 'wise men', evidence which is not very convincing. Before the latter part of it could be admitted it would be necessary to prove that the Druids really were wise men, a point which we fear would present some difficulty unless we regard acuteness as equivalent to wisdom. The evidence for the presence of snakes in the wood rests on no such shadowy foundation. For a long time the place has had an evil reputation in that connection, and what was said of it a hundred years ago we know to be true today.

We can account for what may be said about Wistman's Wood being the haunt of those creeping things from which man instinctively shrinks, but it may yet be worth remembering that there is a kind of analogy between the picture of this ancient wood on the Dart and that which is presented in Scandinavian mythology. In the groves of Wistman the snakes lie at the roots of the oaks where the latter thrust themselves from the hollows, half-filled with dead and decaying leaves. In the Northern heathen tradition we find the earth supported by the ash Yggdrasil, the stem of which passes through it, one of its roots standing over Nifleim, the abode of death, where it is constantly gnawed by the serpent Nidhogg.

The worship of the serpent was a recognition of his power, and this was once acknowledged in a great part of the world. In the Hindoo mythology we hear of a being whose heel was wounded by a serpent, while in return a mortal wound was inflicted on the reptile. Among scattered tribes in Africa serpent worship has also been found, and that it was the worship of the Evil One, and a relic of the earliest times, there can be no doubt.

The larger snakes, which are known locally as longcripples, are not dangerous; it is the small adder, or viper, that carries poison in its sting. Speaking generally, it cannot be said that snakes are plentiful on Dartmoor. A man may very well tramp over the hills for ten or fifteen miles for days together and not meet with one, and if he should do so it is quite certain that the reptile will endeavour to escape him. I have heard a few stories about snakes springing at people from hedges, but such an incident has never come within my experience, and I am inclined to believe that they were suggested by a sudden chance appearance of the reptile. There is no danger to be apprehended from snakes on Dartmoor. They will not attack unless interfered with, and only then if they find they cannot escape. In walking over parts of the moor where the heather is of higher growth than usual a man might, of course, inadvertently set foot upon a snake, and if it could not glide away it would naturally turn upon him. One of my loved companions of a former day, my terrier Hexworthy Snap, made short work of these reptiles. He had no fear whatever, and it was only for him to set eyes upon a snake and it was soon rendered harmless. He is now lying at the foot of a craggy hill on the edge of the moor over which he rambled so many miles with me, and one who is near me as I write.

But it does not always happen that the rambler on Dartmoor possesses a dog which knows how to attack a snake properly. If he does not, let him provide himself with a good ash rod, and then, if he be nimble — and the charm does not fail — he will be secure. Immediately an adder is seen a circle must be drawn round it with the rod, and the reptile will find it impossible to leave it. I do not vouch for this; I am only repeating what Dartmoor people used to say. Here is another charm, which, however, is not so much for the rambler as for the rider. If one's horse should chance to be stung by an adder, all that need be done is to place a collar made of ash twigs round his neck; he will then take no hurt. As this likewise applies to cattle and sheep, it should also commend itself to the moormen. The puzzle, when in the more remote parts of the moor, is to find the collar. When found — it will not be necessary to follow Captain Cuttle's advice — use it.

4

Stories of the Stones

It is only to be expected that objects such as stone monuments, the origin of which was not understood by the peasantry, should in time come to have stories attached to them in explanation of their meaning. We have already seen that they were once supposed to be the work of a race of men of great stature and strength, and that some are still found to bear names indicative of this. Stonehenge, the most striking of our British monuments, was, as we have stated, formerly known as the Giants' Dance, and though there is no stone circle on Dartmoor of that name, yet the numerous examples of those objects to be seen there, together with the evidence of a former belief in the existence of giants, show that in the minds of men the two were connected. That stories of dancing should belong to the circles is easily explained, for when the noon-day sun pours its fierce rays upon the ground, the currents of air impart to all objects near it the appearance of a quivering motion, as is the case when things are seen through the heated air rising from a fire. In course of time, the giants were partly forgotten, but the stones standing on the heath, and often appearing to move tremulously, were a constant reminder of the merrymakers who tripped lightly round the maypole on the village green, and the story underwent a change. It was no longer suggested that the stones represented a dance of giants, but one of youths and maidens, and it was usually explained that the reason of their having been transformed into these monoliths was that they had so far forgotten themselves as to indulge in their pleasant pastime on a Sunday. But the first idea was nearer the truth, for it is probable that the men who set up the circles were of a strong and hardy race.

On Stall Moor, not far from the Erme, is a good example of a stone circle, the best, indeed, on Dartmoor, for nearly the whole of the stones are standing, and it is not a restoration. It is sometimes called The Dancers, and also Kiss-in-the-Ring, and the usual story is related of it, with the addition that the dancers ran over the heath after one of their number, and in proof of this a long line of stones extending from the circle is pointed to. Another monument to which a story attaches also bears two names, or, it may be said three, since one of them appears in two forms. This is the ring known as the Nine Stones, near Belstone, but which is sometimes referred to as the Nine Maidens. But the latter is only a corruption of the ancient form of the former. The Celtic word for stone is maen, and as pronounced by an Englishman, would readily become maiden. Thus the Nine Maidens would simply mean the Nine Stones. But there is evidently some confusion here, for the Celtic pronunciation of maen is as though it were spelt mine, and I am inclined to think that an earlier form of the name was the Maen (or Mine) Stones, a repetition, it is true, but yet one that we can understand. I am led to think this from the fact that the circle does not consist of nine stones only, but of seventeen. Thus it is more correctly described by its third name, which is the Seventeen Brothers, who, according to the story, were turned to stone.

On the slope of Cosdon, above Sticklepath, a monument formerly existed, a portion of which was known as the Eight Rocks which it used to be said, and certainly with truth, might be seen to dance immediately they heard the sound of the bells of South Tawton. Other circles there are on the moor to which also attach stories of the kind we are considering, and others again of which nothing appears to be related. Some have fallen and a few have been 'restored', so that Dartmoor can show not only stone monuments of the dim and misty past possessing great interest but also nineteenth and twentieth century erections possessing comparatively little.

It is not always that the circles are associated with dancing. On the slope below Siddaford Tor are two of these objects closely adjoining and which bear the name of the Grey Wethers. These stones, according to a story I gathered in the neighbourhood many years ago, were once boys, who had made their way to this remote spot for the purpose of 'playing ball', though what the game actually was I could not discover. This, in itself, is, of course, innocent enough, but unfortunately they chose the wrong day. They went to play on a Sunday, and were punished by being turned into stone. A similar fate befell some men who also went forth to enjoy themselves on what should have been their day of rest, and in this case it is probable that, like the youths and maidens, they engaged in dancing. They chose a hill near the head waters of the Wella Brook for their sports, and we may presume that all went well for a time. Then suddenly their revels were brought to an end, and in place of a gay company only senseless lumps of granite dotted the sward. The event is commemorated in the name of the hill, which is called Pupers, a corruption, it is supposed, of pipers, and these, together with the merrymakers, may still be seen. It is noticeable that in these stories the punishment inflicted is death, as in the case of the man "that gathered sticks upon the Sabbath day", as related in the Book of Numbers.

A former superstition respecting the stones of the circles and rows was that they could not be counted accurately; that however many times a person might try to do so the result would be different in each case. It is quite possible that there have been occasions when people who have endeavoured to ascertain the number of stones composing a monument may have found it impossible to get their several attempts to agree, but we think that this is in consequence of an unsuitable hour having been chosen for the purpose. After a ploughing match dinner or a harvest supper would be a poor time, for instance.

It will be seen that many of the stone monuments bear names, but this does not apply only to erections of ancient date. On Black Down, in the parish of Mary Tavy, are some groups of comparatively modern stones which serve the prosaic, but exceedingly useful purpose, of marking the edge of the road where it runs along a steep slope, and two of these have names. One group is known in the locality as Peggy's Four Men, and another, and much larger one, as Annie Pinkham's Men. But neither these nor the bond-stones come within the scope of our present remarks.

In former days when antiquaries were prone to regard not only the megalithic remains, but certain naturally formed rocks, as having served some purpose connected with Druidical worship or divination, the logan, or rocking-stone, received a considerable share of their attention. These are found in different parts of Dartmoor, and it does not require much discernment to feel assured that art has had nothing to do with them. One of these, known as the Ruggle Stone, may be seen near the village of Widecombe-in-the-Moor. Once upon a time — this is a safe way of beginning a story when one does not know the date of it — a stranger stopped at the little inn and inquired the way to this stone, of whose wondrous logging-power he had heard. A villager offered to show him the way, and together they went to the spot. The stranger viewed the huge block with much curiosity, and at length placed his hands upon it and endeavoured to rock it. But although he used all his strength he was unable to move it a hair's breadth; it remained as fixed as a mountain.

"What be 'bout?" asked the rustic. "Daun' think to mak'n loug, do 'e?"

"To be sure I do," replied the stranger. "That is what I am come for."

"You may heave to'n so much as you mind to, but you wan't get'n to do't. There's aunly wan thing'll get'n to move."

"And what is that?"

"The kay o' Widecombe Charch. He'll move with he aisy enough, but there bant nort else in the world that'll make'n to."

There are logans in Lustleigh Cleave, one being called The Nutcrackers, another of similar name on Rippon Tor, also at Stinka Tor, Siddaford, Bellaford, and other places, but, unlike the Ruggle Stone, none require a church key to move them.

Of the cromlech, or as that monument is now usually called by antiquaries, the dolmen, there are only a few examples in the Dartmoor district. The finest of these is the well-known Spinsters' Rock, which is to be seen in a field on Shilston Farm, about two miles from Drewsteignton. If in the story concerning it, which is to the effect that it was erected one morning by three spinsters, or spinners, the three Fates are to be recognised, as has been suggested, it would appear that a Saxon legend has attached itself to a Celtic monument, and there is nothing improbable in this. The farm on which the dolmen stands evidently derived its name from it, Shilston being a corruption of Shelfstone, which appears in Domesday as Selvestan. Another tradition attributed the erection of the dolmen to three young men, but this is not now heard in the locality. But that there was once an object of this kind to be seen in that part of the moorland district, and that it was reported to have owed its erection to three of the male sex, certainly appears to be the case. On the common near Kes Tor, and not far from the well-known menhir, is a stone having all the appearance of a supporter of a capstone, and bearing the name of the Three Boys. Its story is lost now, and speculations concerning the meaning of the name are valueless, but we might not be entirely wrong if we saw in it a reference to those three of whom it was said "by these were the nations divided in the earth after the flood".

This number is found in connection with other objects on Dartmoor. The cairn, or huge heap of stones, marking a burial place, is in many instances seen in groups of three. One hill takes its name from this circumstance, being known as Three Barrows, or, as it is rendered in an old document, Threberis. The barrow, though it served the same purpose as the cairn, was not of similar construction. The former is a mound of earth; the latter consists entirely of stones heaped upon one another, sometimes to a considerable height. On Dartmoor, where stone is abundant, cairns are numerous, while barrows are not often seen. In districts where there is a scarcity of stone the barrow was common, as in the case of the Wiltshire Downs. But it is safe to say that the term 'barrow' as we now understand it never appears in the names of burial mounds on Dartmoor. The earlier forms of the word exhibit the Saxon 'burghe', or 'borough', and this was applied to the stone heaps we now call cairns. The moorman invariably calls them 'burrows', and this has, in one case at least, led to a few scattered rocks, once probably a rabbit burrow, being regarded as the remains of an ancient mound and receiving a name in accordance with the idea. That these heaps should at one time have been supposed to be the graves of giants is not surprising when we consider their immense size. Eastern Whitaburrow on Brent Moor is ninety yards in circumference and twelve yards in height. This does not occupy the greatest area, but there is no finer example on the moor, since it was evidently completed, which all do not appear to have been, and has not suffered at the hands of the spoliator.

The opening of some of these burial mounds has resulted in the discovery of various articles indicative of their purpose, and in a barrow on Hameldon the late Mr. C. Spence Bate found the bronze blade and amber pommel of a dagger, the latter studded with small gold pins. It was customary among certain early races of men when burying their dead to place the weapons of the deceased by his side, in order that he might not be left defenceless in the spirit-land. In the primitive graves on Dartmoor these weapons are almost invariably of flint, and the discovery of such articles made of bronze is much rarer. Of course, the use of the latter would in general point to a more recent period than would flint, but at the same time it is by no means improbable that for a time the use of the two was contemporaneous, and that flint was used on Dartmoor down to a period much nearer to our own than is usually supposed. In conjunction with Mr. Spence Bate, who was an enthusiastic antiquary, I made some investigations in this direction in southern Dartmoor.

Several stories are related concerning the opening of cairns, the moral of which seems to be that these objects should not be meddled with. Dreadful noises have been heard when they have been dug into, and ill-luck has overtaken those who have thus desecrated the resting places of the dead. Several of the cairns and mounds on Dartmoor bear names. We have already mentioned the Giant's Basin, and besides this there are among others the Lord Mayor's Castle, the Heap o' Sinners, and the Ring o' Bells, the latter being either a despoiled, or uncompleted, cairn, and consisting merely of a low circular bank of stones and turf.

A monument which is found in Cornwall, but not on Dartmoor, is the tolmen, or holed stone. But while there is nothing of the kind in the latter — that is to say, no stone having an artificial hole in it of the sort associated with the monument in question — there is at all events one that nature has fashioned. In the bed of the North Teign is the oft-visited Tolmen, a large block of stone through which wind, gravel, and water have pierced a hole sufficiently large for a man to pass through. A story told in the locality speaks of children having formerly been brought here to be 'christened'. This may be the remains of a tradition showing that the stone was once put to some use in connection with certain ceremonies of which lustration formed an important part, or it may, which is more probable, have been fastened upon this stone in recent times in consequence of the older antiquarians speaking of it as a tolmen. On Staple Tor, above the Walkham, is a rock curiously supported on two others, and the aperture formed beneath it having attracted the attention of an antiquary who visited the tor over a hundred years ago, he immediately pronounced it to be a tolmen, but on reflection changed his mind, and expressed the opinion that it was designed as "a kind of moral touchstone" by the Druids. Such conjectures are amusing, and that is all that can be said for them. Tolmens were once thought to be resorted to by people troubled with certain diseases, and a superstition of this kind was formerly attached to the Whooping Rock on Easdon Tor, on the common near Manaton and North Bovey. Children were taken there to be cured of the whooping cough; hence the name of the rock. But this was not supposed to be affected by any virtue possessed by the rock — which thereby differed from a tolmen — but by the sheep which gathered there, it being thought that the presence of those animals would effect the desired cure. By others the rock was said to have received its name in consequence of the noise made by the wind rushing through some aperture between it and those it rested on. It is convenient to be offered the choice of two explanations. One is quite as probable as the other.

❋❋❋❋❋

5

Treasure Seekers

A belief has always existed among the peasantry that treasure had at some early time been hidden in cairns and kistvaens, and this doubtless arose from the discovery in some of them of ornaments that had been placed with the dead, more particularly in Saxon grave-mounds. The kistvaen being in the form of a small stone chest would appear to the peasant, who did not know its true purpose, as having been a receptacle for something of value, and they are still referred to on Dartmoor as money-boxes. Those who first despoiled them would, of course, soon become aware of their true purpose, but later, when the evidences of an interment had disappeared, this would cease to be generally understood. The average size of a kist, which on Dartmoor is composed of slabs of granite, is rather under two feet in width, while its length is often less than three. This was sufficiently large to receive the corpse, which, as discoveries of skeletons in various parts of the country have shown, was laid on its side, the knees being drawn up nearly to the chin. But this mode of sepulture would, of course, be unknown to the peasant, and the size of the kist would, therefore, hardly suggest the notion of a coffin. Often the body was first cremated, and it was simply an urn of baked clay containing the ashes that was deposited in the kist, and this appears to have been the usual manner adopted by the race of men who once inhabited Dartmoor.

But our Devonshire hill-country men, although they have a sort of belief that treasure was formerly concealed in the kists, or at all events are not ignorant that such was once said to be the case, would hardly expect to find such within a kist now should he chance to come upon one that had not been opened. It is true he is a little suspicious of the antiquary when he sees him carefully searching these ancient burial places, for he finds it difficult to understand why such pains should be taken if nothing more than a few pieces of flint, or fragments of pottery, are to be the reward. But, on the other hand, the discovery of anything of value has never come within his own experience, or that of his neighbours, and it is therefore hardly to be wondered at that his interest in such matters is very much less than it might be had he something more tangible than mere report before him. Many of them, indeed, accept the explanation that kists were formed to receive the dead, while at the same time entertaining a notion that treasure may have been buried with them. Forty years ago I knew a man who had lived on Dartmoor all his life, who regarded the kists as burial places, and always spoke of them as graves; and I have known those who so firmly believed that they were repositories of treasure that they have taken the trouble to search for it. But I never knew one who found any.

In most of the stories relating to searches in these ancient graves ill-fortune overtakes the spoliators. The lesson would, therefore, seem to be that it is unwise to meddle with them. But lessons are often very hard to learn when they indicate a course that seems to conflict with self-interest, and as the Dartmoor man is the same as other men in this connection, he has always been undeterred by the sad fate of those who have desecrated the resting places of the dead. What has prevented him from doing likewise is the belief, either that somebody has already rifled the kist and carried off the treasure, or that there never was any in it.

By the side of the green path that runs across Tor Royal Newtake, and forms a direct way between Princetown and Hexworthy, is a fine example of a kistvaen, which bears the name of the Crock of Gold. It was probably rifled of its contents long ago, for when my attention was drawn to it many years since nobody remembered it in any other condition than that in which it then was. It is not unlikely that its name was given to it merely as a matter of fancy by those living in the locality, as in other similar instances met with on the moor; or, it may be that a cinerary urn was once discovered in it, the first sight of which would assuredly cause the searcher to believe that he had unearthed a vessel containing treasure. Guineas are the coins usually spoken of by the moormen as forming the hoards supposed to have been concealed in the kists. In fact, all old coins that they may have heard of being found on the moor are so designated by them. I am acquainted with a moorman who once found what were apparently some ancient bronze coins, but which he described to me as 'base guineas'. In this belief he threw them away, and thus something that might have proved of interest, and possibly of value, was lost. There is a story of a considerable sum of money having been found in some kistvaens near

Widecombe, though whether it was in guineas or not the rural chroniclers have not informed us. The little mounds beneath which the kists were buried, and which it was usual to throw up over them, attracted the notice of a certain man who dwelt in the neighbourhood, and he conceived the idea that they marked places where treasure was concealed. Why anybody desirous of hiding money should, after burying it, attract attention to the spot by heaping a mound over it he did not stop to ask himself; it was sufficient for him that he considered he had discovered places where money was likely to be found, and he determined to possess himself of it. One version of the story gives it that he was the vicar of Widecombe, and if so it is probable that he intended to give to the church the wealth he hoped to gain, for we can hardly suppose he would design to keep such 'filthy lucre' for himself. The feeding of his flock would, of course, be his first consideration, and he would endeavour to do that at whatever pains to himself. But be this as it may, the treasure seeker set out, taking some of his workmen with him to assist in the good work. His endeavours proved successful, and when the task of rifling the graves was over he found himself the possessor of considerable wealth. If it be true that he was the parson, we can imagine what beneficent schemes for the well-being of his parishioners suggested themselves to him as he viewed the heaps of gold coins that somebody had thoughtfully hidden long ago. It was bread cast upon the waters — or gold deposited on Dartmoor — and he had found it after many days. But his was not a lasting joy; for no sooner was the whole of the treasure spread before him than a terrific peal of thunder shook the house to its foundations. It tottered and fell. Once more was the gold buried, and this time the wealth-seeker with it. It is said that a strong smell of brimstone came from the ruins, and this, too, by those who maintain that the searcher really was the parson. But a parson and — brimstone? There must be some mistake.

Tradition speaks of an old squire who once lived at Longbetor, on the Wapsworthy Brook, a stream that falls into the Tavy at Hill Bridge, and who was reputed to be the possessor, if not of great wealth, at least of a very comfortable sum. But when he died he left nothing behind him, and the inference was that he had buried his money. Search failed to reveal it, however, and all that is now to be seen are the scanty ruins of his house and a part of his oven. Somewhere near there may be a chest containing his store of guineas, but we cannot be certain. Not far from the squire's house is the mound called the Frenchmen's Grave, which also has been searched, and with a like result. On the southern verge of the moor is an ancient barton, once the abode of a family of note, but now a farmhouse. It is one of those places that appear as though their builders intended them to stand for ever. Massive arched doorways of granite, and mullions of the same enduring stone, are interesting features, and wide hearths, and huge but low chimneys. Quite near to it is the site of the chapel, a building probably pulled down, since the remains of its walls show it to have been as strongly built as was the house itself, and here the occupier, with whom I was acquainted, showed me where he had searched for the riches of the ancient owner, which he thought it not unlikely had been hidden within it. But "the old fella's money", as he expressed it, was not to be found. Another of my Dartmoor friends of a former day — Will Mann, of Hexworthy — was once persuaded that he should find a 'money-box' under a certain rock, and, after a deal of hard work, contrived to move the latter from its place. But not only was he doomed to disappointment, but to still harder labour than before, for the farmer, on whose land the rock was situated, made him replace it.

The treasure which tradition tells us is buried on Ringmoor Down, and in the field at Fardle, near Cornwood, does not seem to have attracted much notice. This, perhaps, is hardly to be wondered at, seeing that no clue exists to guide the searcher to the part of the down or field in which it lies. In this way it seems to be as securely guarded as the gold buried at Dolbury and Cadbury in another part of Devon, over which, according to an old writer, a fiery dragon keeps watch. But something was once found on Ringmoor Down, notwithstanding, although it was not a treasure of great value. It was in the days when a drop of good spirit occasionally found its way into the farmhouses at a low price, consequent upon there. having been no charge upon it for duty. One, Tom Penny, who greatly interested himself in supplying the farmers round Meavy and Sheepstor with what they required in this direction, having received an order for a certain quantity to be delivered at Brisworthy, near Cadaford Bridge, set out for that place one evening after dark carrying the spirit with him in a bladder. Now it was an arrangement that he was never to take it direct to the house, for prying eyes were sometimes about, and Tom's visits there might have aroused suspicion, for the trade in which he was engaged was known to others besides his customers. It was his practice to lay it in the grave, as he said; in other words, to conceal it in a kistvaen near Legis Tor, which was not far from the house. It was not made to be put underground, he had said to the farmer when devising his plan; but never mind that, it would soon rise again; spirits always did. When Tom neared the tor on this particular evening looking cautiously about him, his sharp eyes detected something moving among the rocks. Dropping to the ground he kept watch, and presently saw the head and shoulders of a man dimly outlined against the little light that still lingered in the sky. He waited for a time, and then seeing by the man's actions that he was not observed, crept stealthily away. When he knew that intervening ground hid him from sight he rose to his feet, and setting off at a run speedily reached Brisworthy.

The farmer was surprised to see him.

"Don't ask no questions," said Tom hurriedly. "Take this and put it away, and give me the empty bladder. Never no more in the grave, though. We'll find another place in the future."

As soon as Tom had received the bladder again he turned away, and after stopping for a few moments at the water spout, set out for the tor as rapidly as he had come. When he drew near to it he slackened his pace, and peered through the gloom.

"I knew I was right," said Tom to himself. " 'Tis old Parnell. Thinks he's got me, I s'pose. But he'll find himself mistaken."

He moved forward among the rocks, and, reaching the kist, carefully laid the bladder within it. Then, after concealing it with moss, he turned to go.

"Stop, Tom Penny," exclaimed a voice. "I see you there."

"That's more than I can say about you, Mr. Parnell," returned Tom. "But whatever are you doing out this way?"

"Looking after you, Tom Penny," answered Parnell, coming forward. "So you've left something for Briseny, have you."

"I have left nothing here for Briseny," said Tom.

"Come, come; it is of no use your denying it. I saw you hide something among the rocks there. It is spirits, and I think you must own you are fairly caught."

"I'll own to no such thing," answered Tom.

"Wait a minute," said Parnell.

He went down on his knees, and pulling aside the moss presently fished the bladder out of the kist.

"It's all up, Tom Penny," he cried. "I've got you fair this time."

"How's that?" asked Tom.

"Because you'll have to account for the possession of this spirit."

"I have left no spirit here."

"What do you call this, then?" demanded Parnell.

"Better see for yourself," said Tom.

Parnell untied the string, and smelt the contents of the bladder. This he repeated, and then tasted them.

"Why, it's water!" he cried.

"Who's caught fair now, Mr. Parnell," asked Tom. "But there; you have no occasion to complain. You have a part of what's required for brewing grog. One man has got the spirit, and you've got the water."

There was a time when the commons on the western side of Dartmoor extended from what is now the fringe of the waste to the Tamar, and included in this area were the downs of Roborough and Buckland. In one part of the latter, and close to the Tavy, is the cave of the Virtuous Lady, in which a certain abbot of Tavistock once discovered a valuable treasure. Its existence was revealed to him in a dream, and he lost no time in setting out for the spot. Unlike the treasure-seeker of Widecombe, he took no one with him, deeming it safer that there should be no witnesses of his hoped-for discovery. In these circumstances it is not probable that he designed to hand over to the abbey what he might be so fortunate as to find. He might very well argue that the abbey was rich, while he, the abbot, was poor. Of course he had a perfect right to consider himself poor; every man has if it suits him. He had his declining years to think of, when he might be unable to discharge the onerous duties an abbot was called upon to perform. Those were not the days of old-age pensions and insurance-cards, and consequently a snug little lump in the shape of a treasure which somebody had been good enough to hide and forget would enable a poor old abbot to provide himself with a few comforts in his latter days.

Full of pleasant anticipations he mounted his palfrey and set out for the cave. So impatient was he that he rode at a pace that astonished everybody whom he passed on the way. It was so unseemly, they thought, for an abbot to be in a hurry. On reaching the Tavy he forded it without difficulty and rode straight to the cave. As soon as he saw it his heart gave a great bound. It was as he had beheld it in his dream, and the few doubts that had previously troubled him were no longer felt.

He found the treasure, and it was of far greater value than he had dared to hope for. When he had unearthed the whole, a quantity of rich and rare gems, and heaps of gold coins glittered on the floor of the cave. It was some considerable time before he finished stowing the precious stones about his person, and placing the money in a bag, which he secured to his back. When the task was completed he issued from the cave, and after numerous attempts contrived to climb upon his palfrey's back. Then he rode off to the ford.

It would be more correct to say that he rode to the spot where he expected to find the ford. There was none to be seen now. While he had been engaged in securing the treasure the Tavy had become a roaring torrent, heavy rains having fallen on the moor. Had the abbot been in his usual senses he would have seen the madness of attempting to cross the swollen river. But he was intoxicated with joy, and had only one thought — to get home with his treasure. Heedlessly he guided his palfrey into the flood, and in another instant was being carried swiftly along by the raging waters. A few moments later a riderless steed, which had been swept into a tiny bay, might have been seen climbing up the low bank. The abbot, weighed down by his gold, lay at the bottom of the river.

It is pleasing to turn away from so much that is disappointing, and to be able to record a real find of treasure, if not exactly on Dartmoor, at least very near to it. Towards the close of the year 1827 three labourers engaged in enlarging a potato cave, for Mr. Splatt, of Brixton, came upon a valuable service, consisting of fifteen silver-gilt dishes and

Kistvaen, near Thornworthy.

seven plates, the rim of each being engraved with the arms of Sir Christopher Harris. Both the Crown and Mr. Splatt made claims in respect of this treasure-trove, but abandoned them in favour of Mr. John Harris, a descendant of Sir Christopher, on the story of the plate being unfolded. For nearly two hundred years it had lain where it had been concealed by the representative of the Harris family during the Civil War, the secret dying with him. Much of it was made from silver brought home as spoil when the Armada was scattered, and bore hallmarks of the years 1599, 1600, and 1601. The service was subsequently purchased by Mrs. Cator, of Cirencester, a descendant of the family, who offered it for sale, and in 1911 it was disposed of at Christie's to a Mr. Crichton for £11,500.

A few flints, or a bit of pottery, or other relics of primitive times, may give a great deal of pleasure to the antiquary, as they did to a friend of mine who once unearthed a kist near Thornworthy, but there are few, I venture to think, who would not be equally well-pleased at discovering some hidden Armada silver — perhaps a little more.

6

Spectral Horses and Hounds

From the time when "Sir Tristram and Sir Percival sped o'er the weary wold" to the day when Tom Pearse's grey mare dropped on Widecombe Hill, the horse has figured in legendary lore, and on Dartmoor, that happy hunting ground, the hound has also had its part in peasant story. Spectral horses have been seen stalking over the heath by the light of the moonbeams struggling though the mist, and colts have suddenly appeared in the path of the wayfarer, only to become invisible with equal rapidity. In the legend of Childe of Plymstock, which an old writer found current in the forest three hundred years ago, the hunter's steed figures prominently. The story is apparently of Saxon times, and therefore not of such great antiquity as many of the Dartmoor traditions, but it nevertheless speaks of a sufficiently early period. In the legends of the Wish Huntsman, Diamond Lane, and the Haunted Pool, the horse is also one of the chief features, as in others that we propose to notice. The horse and the hound appear also in the place-names of Dartmoor, but this does not show a traditionary connection between the animals and the places or objects. They are simply names that have been given to the latter in comparatively recent times, or in one or two instances are the result of corruptions. Thus we have Horse Ford, Horse Hole, the Horse Path, White Horse Hill, and Horse Pit; all evidently modern. Hound Tor occurs twice, this being the name of a small tor in the neighbourhood of Cosdon, and also of a large one in the parish of Manaton. It so happens that the former is one of the boundary marks between the forest and the surrounding commons, and it is consequently mentioned in the Perambulation of 1240. There the form of the name of this tor at that time is preserved, and we find it to be Hundetorre. 'Hunde' may mean 'hound', or it may be equivalent to something else the signification of which is now lost, the sound of the word only having remained. That such has been the case in other instances is certain. Local pronunciation has often entirely altered the meaning of a word. A Devonshire archæologist once spoke of an old stone cross as Hospit Cross, the name, of course, being suggestive of hospitium, as though it had once stood near, or marked the site of, a resting place. When engaged on my book descriptive of the crosses of the moorland borders I made some enquiries into the matter, and found that the cross took its name from an adjoining field, which was called Horse Pit — locally Hoss Pit — in consequence of a farmer's horse having been buried there.

Mr. William Burt, who wrote the notes to Carrington's poem on the moor, states that the moor pony is indigenous, and almost in a state of nature. Certainly they are, as Cottle says, among "the wildest forms that breathe" on Dartmoor, and very strong and hardy. Mr. Burt relates an incident concerning one which some men were endeavouring to catch for Captain Cotgrave, who was in charge of the war prison at Princetown from 1808 till 1813. The animal, on being singled out from a herd on Bear Down, mounted some rocks, and one of the men rode up the hill to try to secure it. To the great surprise of the captain, who probably knew much less the ways of Dartmoor ponies than his assistants, the animal evaded capture by leaping completely over the man and his horse. According to some of the stories related of these animals, it has been found impossible to secure them, not because of any exhibition of agility, although such was no doubt exercised, but in consequence of their seeming power to render themselves invisible. They have been observed, perhaps, behind a bank, and those in search of them have carefully noted the spot, and crept towards them, as it seemed, unobserved. But on reaching the place nothing was to be seen of them; they had completely vanished. It certainly is a fact that these animals do possess the faculty of speedily finding a place of concealment, and so mysterious has their exercise of this sometimes appeared that it is not surprising that in an earlier day this was thought to be due to other than natural powers. Stories told to me when I was a child spoke of horses without heads being seen at night in the grounds of Parke, at Bovey Tracey. When the moon shed a faint light upon the sward, these uncanny creatures would appear from out the deep shadow cast by some stately tree, to the great terror of the passer-by, who was literally unable to make head or tail of what he saw.

The horses that draw the coach of bones of Lady Howard, the wife of four husbands, are described as high mettled animals and of a jet black. In the dead of night the coach was formerly to be heard rattling through the streets of Tavistock on its way to the moor, but I have met nobody who has been disturbed by it lately. Nor have I heard of her ladyship being seen doing penance in the form of a hound to which she was long ago condemned, and which was to last till the world came to an end. Horses and hound appear to have ceased their nightly journeys. Acetylene lamps and hooters have, perhaps, rendered the roads distasteful to them.

But this is not the case with the black colt of the peaty hollow that people call Cranmere Pool. Though it does not seem that he is seen in its neighbourhood so frequently as of yore, yet it has not altogether deserted the spot. Those who had not heard the story would never suspect, on seeing a black colt on their way to or from the hollow, that it might be the spirit of Binjie Gear, condemned to wear that form by a council of parsons, who, however, were unsuccessful in their efforts to effect the transformation until one of them addressed the hapless spirit in Arabic. But so it is; one never knows what one may meet with when one goes bog-trotting on Dartmoor.

Another strange sight, once to be seen on certain parts of the moor borders, would also appear, like Lady Howard's coach to be a thing of the past. I have never met anyone who has witnessed it, but that this has been the experience of some must be the case, otherwise we should know nothing about it. I allude to the spectral funeral procession, which is reported to have been seen at different times on the moor. The account given by one witness, of whom I know nothing except that he was called William, though usually referred to as 'Old Billy', is coherent enough, and I know of no reason why it should not be received as readily as any other.

" 'Twas up 'long 'leb'n o'clock," said Billy, "an' though there was a bit of a moon, couldn' see much on for clouds. Still, 'twas fairly lightish like 'cos o' the snaw, which was daip, sure 'nough. 'Twardn' usual for me to be out so late, I needn' tell 'e, so I stapped out so well's I could, wantin' to get home, daun' 'e see. Well, I'd just got clear o' the fuz brake, an' was out 'pon th' aupen, when – Oh, my days! I shall never forget it. I seed it so clearly as I can see you now. There 'twas, a gert black hearse, drawed by four black hosses, movin' across the snaw, an' all so quiet as the grave. I feel'd my blid rin cold, an' aich moment expected to heer my name cal'd out, an' be told I was wanted. I could see wan' drivin', and another sittin' by the side o'n, but they didn' sim to take no notice o' me. I couldn' move if they had a cal'd me. They passed on an' presently I couldn' see no more o' mun. I was so sober's a judge, an' 'tis so true as I'm heer."

But notwithstanding his repeated assertions of the truth of his story, there were several who were a little sceptical about it. But in a few days they began to view the matter in another light. It was discovered that the better-class farmers in the locality had suddenly become rather lavish in offering spirits to everybody who happened to call on them. How had the liquor been brought there? That was the question those who were not among the possessors of the spirit were asking. It was answered by another. What was in the hearse? Nobody had heard of any burial round about, and it was shrewdly guessed that in place of conveying the dead it had brought life into the locality.

Near Didworthy Bridge above South Brent, a narrow track or bridle path leads upward from the right bank of the Avon to the common above Merrifield Farm. This is known as Diamond Lane, and though evidently intended only as a path for pack-horses tradition states that a coach drawn by four horses once passed through it. Such a strange circumstance might naturally prepare us to hear that spectral horses and a great lumbering coach are sometimes to be seen there, but local story has nothing to say about such a ghostly appearance. Possibly, if the place were visited at dead of night, when the moon is on the wane by the seventh son of a seventh son, having but one eye, and with five fingers on his left hand, it might become visible to him. I have never met with anybody qualified to put this to the test, but in an age like the present there is no knowing what may happen.

It may not be generally known that we are indebted to horses for one of our fishes – if tradition speaks truly. The man who eats stewed eels in Whitechapel hardly supposes that the green jelly that he finds so tasty was once hanging from the neck of a horse, but old people on the borders of Dartmoor could have told him so a hundred years ago. It used to be said that the fish in question were formed from the hairs that dropped from the manes of these animals, while they drank from the streams. Whether this was known to Darwin or not I cannot say, but if it be true it is certainly something more than an argument in favour of the theory of evolution, while the old story of proving an eel pie to be a pigeon is nothing compared with it.

The tradition of the Wish Huntsman and his Demon Hounds still lingers on Dartmoor, but in a very shadowy state. The Dewer Stone is regarded as the spot he chiefly favours, and report used to describe him as a swarthy individual who hunted at night, and then only when a storm was raging on the moor. His steed, like those that drew Lady Howard's coach, was black, and his hounds were black also. What they hunted nobody has ever been able to say with certainty, but they appear to have been an extraordinary pack. Their quarry could have stood little chance, for if scent failed, then sight, in all probability, made up for it, since we learn that their eyes glowed like balls of fire and were as big as saucers.

Another animal of the canine species that figures in Dartmoor story is the Black Dog, which haunts the moor, and appears at times like the wandering Jew. I have seen many black dogs on Dartmoor, but that any one of them was the animal in question I should not like to say. But if I have not encountered him one of my old friends did, or thought that he did. I allude to the late Mr. James Perrott, formerly such a well-known figure on the moor, who stoutly maintained that he had seen the animal. It was in full view, and then – in the twinkling of an eye – it mysteriously disappeared. This, however, was an experience which has not been vouchsafed to many. Yet while this is so the dog has often been heard of, particularly on the eastern side of the moor from Widecombe to Gidleigh. The neighbourhood of Soussons and Headland seem to be favourite haunts of the animal, and as there are here extensive warrens, it would appear as though rabbits were the attraction were it not that we can hardly believe that ghosts require to eat. But after all it may be only his sporting instincts that draw him to those places, and the desire for rabbits may not arise from appetite. Those instincts may still survive. It is impossible for me to say; it is rather a question for the Psychical Society to decide.

Northward of Headland Warren the road from Post Bridge to Moreton runs over the commons, and here several examples of hut circles, mixed up with reaves, or low banks of earth and stone, may be seen. Late one night, when the moon, constantly hidden behind drifting clouds, fitfully lighted the moor, Luke Rogers found himself near one of the former, and, being weary, sat down on a stone to rest. He promised himself five minutes, and five minutes only. But the rest was so much needed, for somehow or other Luke's legs had seemed to give way under him during the past half-hour, that it was nearer twenty before he thought about rising. And then that was all that he did. He did not suffer the idea to take practical form, but closing his eyes, sank back against a granite slab.

The next thing of which he seemed to be aware was the presence of some living form within the small circle of stones. He sat up wearily and looked about him. Then he suddenly sprang to his feet, for, within a yard of him was the spectral animal of which he had heard so much, the Black Dog that haunted the moor. With a cry of terror he leaped over

Hut Circle (in foreground), near the Moreton Road.

the stones, and bounded like a deer down the slope.

At his heels was the Black Dog, and Luke fancied more than once that he could feel the brute's fangs fastening upon them. Never in his life had he run so fast, but the fear of being brought down by the spectral animal of which he had heard so much, acted like a spur, and despite the obstacles in his path he ran on at lightning speed. Presently the waters of the Bovey crossed his path, but, without staying to choose a convenient crossing-place, he dashed through the stream, and mounted the hill beyond like an arrow shot from a bow. Next the Teign confronted him, but he bounded across it in an instant. On past the tall menhir to Batworthy Corner, and across the northern Teign, the Black Dog close upon him, and giving him not a moment's respite. Over the swampy flat to Watern Tor. The rocks rise immediately in his path, several times the height of a man, but they present no obstacle to him. Like spring-heeled Jack he mounted into the air, and, alighting on the turf on the further side, was off again with the speed of a hare. The dog followed him, and Luke began to feel that, fast as he could run, and high as he could leap, his pursuer was equal to him. But he held on, skimming the bogs of Cranmere, and pointing straight for Tavy Cleave. Down the narrow defile he went, and then, mounting the hill, again shot up across Wapsworthy Well to Dead Lake Head. Beyond was Great Mis

Tor, but the valley of the Walkham lay between. Luke paused for one instant, and then, with a mighty effort, sprang across the valley, and alighted on the rocks of the tor. He had thrown off the dog now, and would be able to draw breath. But the thought had hardly struck him when a black object was seen dashing over the turf. The dog had leapt across the valley as well.

On again! Past North and South Hisworthy Tors, Eylesbarrow, and on to Erme Head. Over the two Whitaburrows, and down the hill to Huntingdon Cross. Thence on over Pupers and Ryder to Holne Ridge. Down by Combestone Tor to Dartmeet, and, climbing the steep, on over the crest of Corndon. On, on to Ephraim's Pinch and Soussons, and up the valley to Headland. In another minute he had reached the hut circle near the Moreton road, and there Luke dropped exhausted, and his senses left him.

When he came to himself he felt thirsty and feverish, but he speedily rose to his feet and set out for home. On arriving he told his story to his wife.

"Black doug!" she cried, when he had concluded. "Daun' 'e tell me no such ole nonsense. Where was 'e to fust part o' th' aivnin'?"

Luke explained that he had passed an hour or two at the inn at Newhouse.

"Ees, I thought so. An' if you go there again you'll find me arter 'e. You've got away from the doug to be sure, but you wan't get away from me. I'll stick to 'e tighter than he did."

Horses and dogs are early named in connection with Dartmoor. It is said that the Abbot of Buckfast had a stud farm in the forest, and in King John's charter of 1204 permission is given to the men of Devon to "have dogs, bows and arrows, and all other kinds of arm". An old tradition of the moor states that when the bounds of the forest were first marked out they were so fixed that a horse could go from one bondmark to another. In later days horses and dogs have always been closely connected with the moor. At Longbetor, and at Babeny, tradition has it that hounds were at one time kept, and the scratch pack of Tom French, one time of Widecombe, was for a long time spoken of in the locality. My own Gaylass, the grey which carried me many a hundred miles; Brown Bess, which nearly sank under me in a bog on Ringmoor Down; Jack, Tommy, and Surefoot, each awaken within me recollections of Dartmoor, as other steeds do in the minds of other owners that have loved to press the heather. More than one gallant horse and faithful dog lies buried in the Dartmoor country and some, as witness George Templer's beautiful lines, have been celebrated in verse.

❋❋❋❋❋

7

Spirits of the Streams

A river is a thing of beauty when undefiled, and always of service; consequently it has an attraction for men. Like them it has its birth, its youthful vigour, its maturity, and its passing, not to cease to be; but to be received into the boundless ocean after its work is done. It has its impetuous moments, and its periods of calm; at one time full of life, at another serene and tranquil. Dwellers in a district through which a river flows are insensibly drawn towards it, and are impressed by its varying moods. To those of old the Euphrates, the Nile, and the Jordan were mighty facts; in our day even streams more humble exert a similar power, less though it may be in degree.

Dartmoor has been well called a land of streams and the mother of many rivers. From every combe among its numerous hills issues a brook to mingle its waters with others and form rivers that find their way to the Channel or to the Severn Sea. In such a land, where nature is yet supreme, and men live secluded lives, it is to be expected that the feelings with which the river is elsewhere regarded should be intensified, and thus we find that the Dartmoor man looks upon the stream that runs through that part of the waste in which his home is situated as forming no inconsiderable feature of what is to him his little world.

That primitive peoples should have believed that deities presided over rivers was most natural, for, not only were the benefits they brought visible on every hand, but their mighty power was seen every day. To invoke the aid of the river-spirit in certain circumstances, or to endeavour to propitiate it, in others, was part of an early faith, and the thoughts of men in this direction still survive in the stories that attach to streams in various parts of the world.

An early legend connected with West-country streams is that of Tamara, and of this more than one version exists. Risdon has left us one of these, and in this the Tamar and the Torridge figure as rivers only, but a variant speaks of the former as having once been a nymph, the daughter of gnomes, who dwelt in the earth. The beautiful Tamara was beloved by Tavy and Taw, the sons of giants. Being found by her father with her suitors he transformed her into a stream, there being a feud between the earth-men and the giants. The two lovers were afterwards also changed into streams, and Tavy overtook the nymph, but not until she had nearly reached the sea. Taw rushed away to the north and he and the one he loved never met. Risdon gives his story in verse which he received *ex dono amica*, and this also mentions the Ockment and of its meeting with the Torridge.

In the legends of saints we read of springs miraculously caused to burst from the earth, and on Dartmoor we have something analagous to this. It is said that Sir Francis Drake, being concerned at the great scarcity of water in Plymouth, resolved that a supply should be brought into the town. Naturally he turned his thoughts to Dartmoor as being a likely source from whence to obtain this, and lost no time in setting out for that place. Most men would have taken an engineer with them to make plans and inquiry into other important matters connected with such an enterprise, and without which it would be impossible to accomplish it today. But not so Sir Francis. He simply mounted his horse and rode off to the hills alone. In those days no road led over Dartmoor as at present. There was only a green track, marked here and there with a guide-stone, but had there been no path at all it would have mattered nothing to him. However, he seems to have followed the track, and, by-and-by, came to a stony hollow from which trickled a beautifully clear stream. Had the water not possessed this desirable characteristic he would have ridden further, for he knew that the people of Plymouth were only content with the best of everything. But there was no need for him to continue his ride. Here was exactly what was required.

Sir Francis did not dismount. He merely turned his horse's head and rode down the hollow, the brook growing larger and larger as he proceeded. Very soon other brooks ran towards him, some tumbling over the rocks in their haste to join the one he was following, and so it came about that in less than half-an-hour a fine stream was running by his side. But suddenly he stopped. If he went further down the valley how was he going to supply the people who lived on the hill above the Old Town Gate? It could not be done.

It is unnecessary to say that Sir Francis was not the man to hesitate. No sooner did he perceive the trouble ahead of him than he hastened to avoid it. He gave his horse the spur and set off at a gallop along the side of Yennadon Down – and the water followed him! Great was the joy that night in Plymouth when the townspeople saw the gallant Drake ride into their ancient borough with a supply of water at his horse's heels. In after years it was customary to express a wish that the descendants of Sir Francis might never want wine; it is probable that on the night of his arrival from Dartmoor they took good care not to want for any themselves.

Nothing can better define a boundary than a river, and on Dartmoor there are many that serve this purpose. Sometimes they separate one common from another, and in places mark the limits of the forest. This being so, we find mention of them in comparatively early times. Thus in the Perambulation of 1240 the Teign, the Walla Brook, the Dart, the Wo Brook, the Avon, Red Lake, the Erme, the Rattle Brook, and others are named, and in 1291, in a deed of Isabella de Fortibus, Countess of Devon, we have the Tavy, the Walkham, the Plym, the Mew, and the Dean Combe Brook. These names do not appear quite in the forms here given, but the spelling has not changed much. It is, however, noticeable that the Teign is spelled Tyng, which is in accordance with the pronunciation of the moor folk today. The terms 'head' and 'foot', as applied to streams, were also employed as at present, as in Wallebrokshede and Okebrokysfote.

More than one of the rivers named is said to be haunted by a spirit, and among these is the Erme. But in this case it is not a spirit of the kind we should expect to find associated with such a beautiful stream. The Erme has its source in a remote part of the south quarter of the forest, and on its banks there is much to delight the eye, and a great deal that is interesting to the antiquary. Flowing past Erme Pound, an old enclosure formerly used at the time of the drifts, it runs between the bold and precipitous hill of Stalldon Barrow and the lofty height crowned by Three Barrows. Here, on the left bank, are the ancient oaks of Piles Wood, and soon after leaving these it reaches Harford, and flows onward through a deep and wooded valley known as Stowford Cleave. This is the haunt of a dreadful ogre, whose voice is heard at night above the rushing of the stream, crying "more rope! more rope!" Time was when this spirit haunted Stowford, the house above the narrow vale, but for his wickedness was cast out, and condemned to make ropes from the sand of the river. At this task he works incessantly, but his cry is heard only at night, and when the river comes down in a mighty flood from the moor. Then a loud despairing wail rises from the depths of the cleave, and the cry "more rope! more rope!"

Erme Pound: an old drift enclosure.

Below Stowford Cleave the Erme reaches Ivybridge, which is placed in the centre of many beauties. The river still chafes and frets as the boulders it has brought down from the upper valleys in times past check its progress, but beyond these water-worn blocks of granite and the fine frontier height of the Western Beacon, there is nothing to suggest that this sheltered village, surrounded by pleasant meads, is so near the moor. From Ivybridge the Erme flows onward to Ermington, and thence past Flete to Mothecombe, where it falls into the sea. Here it was that Philip, King of Castile, in the reign of Henry VII, was driven by a storm, and lost two of his ships.

Another ogre is connected with the Yeo, a stream that rises on the slope of Rippon Tor, and after flowing through Ashburton, falls into the Dart. This ogre, who so far as I can learn, has not been seen lately, was known as Cutty Dyer, and he seems to have been fond of pulling passers-by into the water. This may at first sight seem rather unkind, particularly as it does not appear that in any instance he was first assailed. But when we come to learn the true circumstances we may perhaps be inclined to modify our opinion concerning him. One night, when the hour in which Shakespeare tells us that "churchyards yawn" was fast approaching, two men might have been seen slowly making their way along the brink of the Yeo. Behind them the old town of Ashburton lay wrapped in slumber, and with the exception of the sound of their footsteps, and an occasional exclamation, the silence was unbroken. Had anyone been abroad at that late hour to notice them he would have seen that something seemed to hinder them from walking with that precision which is generally expected from people on the highway. It may have been that they were firm believers in the rule that there is no beauty in a straight line, but that a succession of curves was much more to be desired; or it is possible that the uncertain light of the moon rendered it difficult for them to see the road. It would also have been noticeable that they frequently stopped, and seemed to be engaged in an argument, one appearing to desire to go in a direction to which the other was altogether opposed.

In the midst of one of these discussions one of them suddenly started back, and a loud yell rang out upon the night.

"Cutty Dyer!" he cried.

His companion grasped his arm, and stared in the direction towards which he pointed.

There, standing in the middle of the Yeo, was the gigantic form of the dreaded ogre. The water was dripping from his garments, and gleamed in the baleful light that shot from the great goggle-eyes of the monster. His black hair hung down over his shoulders in twisted locks that could only be likened to snakes, and his beard of the same colour descended to his belt. Little of his face was visible, but the huge eyes, and the teeth like those of a shark, were quite sufficient to repress any inquisitive desire on the part of the men to see the rest of his features. Transfixed with horror, the two wayfarers stared wildly at those gleaming eyes. Slowly the monster raised his arm, and stretched out his hand towards them. Nearer and nearer it came, until the great fingers touched the shoulder of the nearest. Then the spell was broken, and with a cry of terror the men staggered away from the stream.

Now at first sight Cutty Dyer's conduct does not appear to be very commendable. But, as I have already said, we must know all the circumstances before we can judge in the matter. When we hear that on the following morning one of the wayfarers was found sound asleep in a cucumber frame, partially buried by the broken glass of the top light, and that the other was in the lock-up for having assaulted the constable, we shall perhaps be inclined to think that Cutty Dyer knew what was best for them when he offered to introduce them to his element. His name is perpetuated in Cuddyford Bridge which spans the little stream where he is said to have made his haunt.

Peter Tavy Combe, a charming spot that takes its name from the village near by, was once, if we are to believe the stories, much favoured by the water-spirits. But they were very different spirits to the ogre of the Yeo. Here were to be seen, when the moonlight silvered the little stream that runs through the combe and forms numberless tiny cascades, troops of fairies disporting themselves in a variety of ways. The combe was a fitting place for their gambols, and though their absence may deprive it of one among its many interesting features, there is still left so much that is beautiful that we do not miss it.

Far out over the hills that shelter Peter Tavy Combe is the one-time pool to which we have already referred, the solitary Cranmere, where Binjie roams in the form of a black colt, or, as another story has it, in the shape of an ugly dwarf. Doomed to dip the water from the pool he worked incessantly with the sieve which alone he was permitted to use. Had he not found the sheepskin and wrapped it round his sieve, and so baled out the pool, the inference is that the rambler thither would today have seen it in a condition justifying its name. When the water disappeared Binjie disappeared too, and now there is nothing more to look upon than a hollow in the peat.

The spirit of the Dart, chief river of the moor, is said to claim a heart every year, either in its moorland course, or where it becomes a navigable stream below Totnes. This was once the popular belief, and there are many who still think it true, and, as may well be imagined not without good reason, when the length of the river is considered. When the 'cry' of Dart – the article is often omitted by the moor people – rises from the valley, it is the spirit of the river calling for his prey. Once it claimed two victims in the year. It was when two lovers threw themselves into its flood from the rock in the Buckland Woods, which has ever since been known as the Lovers' Leap.

All the Dartmoor rivers have their 'cry', and this is heard chiefly in the quiet of the evening. Each has its spirit, too; not the fabled demi-god, but one much more real – the spirit of beauty. It was this spirit that claimed the life of the artist years ago. Attracted by the charms of the Ockment, where it runs through the long and deep gorge to the Island of Rocks, he ventured where his foot should not have taken him, and the river received its victim.

In all the Dartmoor streams deep basins are found and these are known as pools. A number of them bear names as Bel Pool, Zeal Pool,

Tan Pool, and the Wishing Pool. What magic influence controls the latter it is impossible to say, but according to the story anyone leaping across it, and expressing a wish while doing so, will have that wish gratified – if he lands safely on the other side. The pool is situated immediately below the meeting of the East and West Glaze, the united stream there forming the boundary between Brent and Ugborough Moors. The visitor to the spot will probably be of the opinion that the most sensible wish that those who attempt to leap across it can express is that they may not fall short of the further bank.

8

Fountains of the Fairies

Fitz's Well, on the Blackabrook.

A lthough the springs on Dartmoor are practically without number only a few have stories attaching to them. They are usually spoken of as wells, though as a matter of fact there is only one true well on the moor, and even that is now within the enclosures belonging to the prison at Princetown. This is known as Fice's Well, a local rendering of its true name – Fitz's Well: It is situated near the Blackabrook, and to the north of the road running from Rundle Stone Corner to Two Bridges. I remember when the well was on the open moor, and the little edifice of granite over it standing in the solitude of the waste presented a quaint and interesting appearance. Not far from it a rude clapper, swept away by a flood in 1873 but since restored by the prison authorities, spans the Blackabrook at a point which was apparently on the track that ran over the moor before the present road was made. On the front of the flat stone that forms the covering of the little edifice is a small panel on which the letters I.F. and the date 1568 are carved in relief.

Why were these stones erected over the well, and who placed them there? These questions are not difficult to answer. The builder there can be no doubt was John Fitz, who, in 1568, was living at Fitzford, near Tavistock. In that year he was granted liberty to convey water to Fitzford, and though this would have nothing to do with the moor, we may imagine that grateful for being able to supply his mansion with water he erected the covering over the well on the Blackabrook as a thank offering, and for the use of travellers passing that way. John Fitz, besides being a man learned in the law also devoted himself to the study of astrology, and was in all probability conversant with the beliefs of Druidism. He might have imagined it possible that this clear spring may have figured in some of their rites, and was thus directed to the choice of it. But if this explanation be not deemed satisfactory tradition comes forward with another which, if not the true one, is at least not wanting in interest.

It happened one day when John Fitz, in company with his lady, was riding over Dartmoor that he lost his way, and, though he made every effort to find it, was utterly unable to regain the track. John Fitz knew what had happened; he had been led astray by the pixies, a race of little beings of which we shall have something to say in another chapter. Versed, as in all probability he was, in charms, it appears that he was unable to hit upon one to extricate him from his present dilemma, and had not fortune favoured him his wanderings would have continued much longer than they did. But at length they reached a beautiful spring, and being hot and thirsty he and his lady dismounted, and drank of the pure water as it bubbled up from the earth. It was a veritable fairy fountain. No sooner had they tasted the water than the power of the pixies over them was gone, and their way was revealed. There was the path they had tried in vain to find while under the spell of the pixies. The magic water of the spring had broken it, and they were free. In thankfulness for the help he had received, John Fitz formed the well and erected the granite covering. The water was long said to possess many healing properties, as well as being a potent charm in all cases of pixy-led travellers.

There is another Fitz's Well on Dartmoor, but, unlike the one on the

Blackabrook, it is not a true well; only a small pool, and usually dry in summer. It is situated within the enclosures of Okehampton Park, and takes its name from the same family, the Fitzes having formerly owned land near by. A story similar to the other is related of it, but the actors in it are not named. Very probably it has been copied from it.

In 1609 a jury presented the bounds of the forest at a court held at Okehampton, and among other boundary marks they mentioned Deadlakehead. The spot is still called by the same name, and the little stream, or lake as it was termed, is known as Deadlake Well. This falls into the Walkham under Great Mis Tor, and the combe through which it runs is just what might be supposed would be chosen as a haunt by the fairies, and, if so, it is probably to them that the water owes its peculiar power. As this is not seen at once, it calls for a little patience on the part of those who put it to the test. If we are to believe the story, the first member of a party reaching the stream and drinking of the water will find a husband or wife, as the case may be, before the end of the year.

A labourer of Harford, having been told that whoever would go to Ducks' Pool and stop there till twelve o'clock at night without being pixy-led would find himself well rewarded by the fairies, inquired of a neighbour where the pool was.

"You must go up the Erme so far as you can follow water, and then you'll find Ducks' Pool 'pon your left hand. But what do 'e want to go there for Simon?"

Simon told him.

"Passel of ole crams," said his neighbour. "I wouldn' believe in such ole nonsense. You wan't get nort from the fairies; there ban't none there."

But Simon was not to be turned from his resolve, and the next evening he set out. Following the instructions given him, he reached the pool just as it was growing dark, and sat down on the edge of it. It was really only a large hollow with a spring in it, the water having been drained from it long before, and not at all the sort of place that fairies would be likely to gather in. But Simon knew nothing of that; indeed, he was hardly concerning himself about the fairies at all. It was the pixies he was thinking of.

An hour passed away, and Simon began to have certain misgivings. What if, after all, his neighbour should be right? He had certainly expected to see some pixies near the pool, and had made a resolve that if he did they should not lead him astray. It was only for him to follow water, he thought, and then he could not fail to reach Harford Bridge, so if he did not suffer himself to be drawn away from that all would be well. But he could see no pixies, and asked himself how that would affect his reward. Would the fairies be inclined to give him one if the pixies did not attempt to draw him away? He began to wish that he had followed his neighbour's advice and remained at home.

Slowly the hours passed, but an end came to his vigil at last. His watch, seen by the light of a match, told him it was twelve o'clock. Not a pixy nor a fairy had he seen.

"They'll call me a proper fool," he said to himself as he replaced the watch in his pocket. "I must ha' been maze to come."

He was about to rise when a sound as of something moving fell upon his ear. His heart beat quickly. Here were the fairies at last. But a glance in the direction whence the sound proceeded showed him that he was mistaken, for the faint light lent by the stars revealed the figure of a man.

Simon got upon his feet.

"You'm out a bit latish," he said.

"Much later than I wished to be, my friend," answered the stranger. "I have lost my way. I left Princetown this afternoon, and have been wandering about ever since. I'd give a sovereign if I could get off the moor."

"Which way do 'e want to go?" asked Simon.

"I am staying at Ivybridge. If I could get to Harford Bridge I should be all right. I know the road from there."

"It's a bargain," said Simon.

The stranger put a sovereign into his hand, and in another minute they were on their way to the Erme.

The next morning Simon's neighbour was waiting for him as he came from his cottage.

"Well, Simon, an' how did 'e get on last night?" he asked.

"Capital, sure 'nough," answered Simon. "I got to Ducks' Pool all right an' stopped till twelve o'clock, an' then all to wance I found this in my hand."

He held up the sovereign and grinned.

"Aisiest money I ever arn'd in my life," he said.

Above Yarner Wood, and on the road from Hey Tor Vale to Manaton, is a spring known as Yarner Wells. The spot is altogether just such a one as we should associate with fairies, and if ever they did visit Dartmoor, surely they must have gathered here. In a place like this we can well imagine it was that the fairies saw the poor man give half the food he possessed, and which he was taking to his home, to one poorer than himself, and in their own delightful way rewarded him for it. When he reached his cottage, thinking to have but a poor supper, he was surprised to find a joint of meat on the table, and on going to his cupboard found it stocked with a number of necessary articles. With joy and thankfulness he looked upon his little store, and blessed the unknown donor. He tried in vain to discover who this was, and could only come to the conclusion that the fairies had put the good things there.

Some kind little fairies watch over the spring of St. Gudula, on the outskirts of Ashburton. They do not bring food and other necessaries to those who make use of the water, but a wondrous power is exercised nevertheless. In cases of weak eyes the water is said to be of great efficacy, and no fairy fountain could be of greater value. The spring bears the name of Gullwell. Another spring was once known to exercise a remarkable power, for it was said, and with truth, that on one occasion it caused a man to see water where he had never beheld it before. It happened that a labourer while engaged in digging near the Forest Inn at Hexworthy, was surprised to find water suddenly bubble up. It increased in volume, and became a perennial spring. Surely the fairies had something to do with that. Peter's Spring is its name, and this it fittingly received from the labourer.

On the borders of the moor quaint-looking wells are seen in several places, as in the village of Widecombe, at Gidleigh, and at Sticklepath; and among other so-called wells on the moor itself, that is springs bearing that name, are Broady Well, Dick's Well, and Wild Tor Well. Tradition does not tell us whether these have any connection with the fairies, but when we look at their crystal waters we can at least say that they are fountains such as we should associate with them.

Close to the boundary between Brent and Ugborough Moors is a small sheet of water bearing the name of Knattaburrow Pool, to which is attached a story. If I were to say it is not a fairy tale, the reader would probably be inclined to disagree with me, notwithstanding that it does not relate to the fairies. It concerns one Peter the Peat-man, a labourer of Ugborough. Peter was fond of boasting of his parish, always telling strangers whom he met where he came from, a patriotic feeling which is to be commended. But if he was proud of being an Ugborough man he was prouder still of being, as he considered, a ladies' man, and firmly believed that none of the fair sex could withstand him. Why he should have so regarded himself is hard to say since he never made any conquests. Peter delighted to take his stand at the churchyard gate on a

Sunday in order that he might be seen by every maid-servant, or other eligible young lady, who attended the service. At such times his smirk raised a smile on the faces of those towards whom his glance was directed, and this he took for a look of admiration. Then Peter was supremely happy.

During summer Peter was in the habit of cutting peat on the moor and being about the only man in the village who engaged in that work, gained the name by which he was usually known. On his way to and from his work he often passed Knattaburrow Pool, and it so happened that one night he had a dream about it. It was on a Sunday night after he had spent a more than usually happy time at the churchyard gate, for he had noticed that one young girl who passed in had looked back at him twice. He dreamed that he saw a beautiful lady standing on the brink of the pool beckoning to him to come to her. Something seemed to tell him, too, that she was possessed of great riches, and altogether a most desirable being with whom to link his fate. Such an opportunity was not to be neglected. He tried to approach her, and – awoke.

That very day he would go to the pool. This was Peter's determination: He was a little puzzled to know what clothes he should wear. Whether he should go in his Sunday best, or in his ordinary working garb. After some reflection he decided upon the former, notwithstanding that he knew it would cause some talk in the village. When he had finished his breakfast he set out, taking with him, as he usually did when going on the moor, a large jar of ale, for he reflected that he might have to wait some time before the lady appeared, and that he would need some refreshment the while. When he arrived at the pool he was pleased that he had been so thoughtful, and, seating himself on the turf immediately proceeded to draw the cork.

The day was hot, and, Peter being thirsty, his attacks upon the beer were long and frequent. The consequence was that in less than half-an-hour the whole of it was gone, and Peter was in anything but a fit state to receive a lady. He closed his eyes and began to doze.

How long he continued in this state he did not know, but when he came to himself and looked about him he quickly discovered that he was not alone. On the further side of the pool a female figure was standing, and her gaze directed towards him.

It so happened that on this morning a party of young people from Brent had arranged to go on the moor whortleberry gathering, and on reaching the vicinity of Knattaburrow Pool one of the girls, who had a desire to see it, had left her companions for a few minutes in order to gratify her curiosity. On reaching it she was surprised to find a man asleep on the bank. Almost at that moment Peter woke up.

"Heer I be," cried Peter, scrambling to his feet. "I was expectin' of 'e."

The girl, who was about to turn away, was reassured on hearing this, supposing that it was someone who intended joining the party.

"I'm an Ugborough man," said Peter, moving towards her; "an' you daun't belong to that parish, I knaw. But there; you bant the wuss for that."

"I should hope not," returned the girl.

"I knaw'd you was comin'. I draimed about 'e."

Peter put on his most endearing look, but it seemed to have an effect upon the girl the reverse of what he intended, for she made a movement as though to go.

"Daun't rin away," cried Peter, "I've a com' out heer a purpose to see 'e. You ought to be proud o' that when you knaw who I be. I'm Peter in there to Ugborough."

The girl had heard of him and consequently did not wonder at his manner of speaking to her.

"You bant zackly like the wan I draimed about," went on Peter still with a smirking look on his face, "but you'm a goodish soort of a maid, and I sim you'll suit me. Us'll go 'long together."

"I must let the other maidens know I'm not going hert pickin' then," said the girl. "Stay here till I come back."

She ran off, leaving Peter in a state of great happiness. He felt confident that he had favourably impressed the girl, and that she would soon return.

"Wish I'd got a drap more beer," he said, looking into the depths of the pool; "I'm most chuckin'."

Had he been looking in another direction he would have seen two young Brent men approaching him. They had come from the whortleberry gatherers' party in place of the girl.

"Ees, 'tis a pity," continued Peter musingly. "But there; her'll gi' me a kiss directly, I daresay, an' that'll make up for 't a bit. But I could ha' drinkt another pint for I'm mortal dry."

"No you bant!" cried the Brent men, rushing forward. "You'm wet enough, Peter!"

The lady-killer in the middle of the pool deemed the remark superfluous.

※※※※※

9

The Pixies

On a beautiful summer evening in the year 1854 I saw my first and last pixy. It was at their well-known haunt on Sheeps Tor. I was very young at the time, but I have nevertheless a recollection of my visit thither. For some time previously I had been plentifully regaled with stories of the little elves, and had been told how they made their home in a small cave on the side of the great tor that rose not far off, and on which I so often looked in wonderment. I had been promised, too, that I should go to the tor and see the cave, and this raised in me the most pleasurable anticipations. It was customary then for everybody who entered the abode of the pixies to leave some offering for the little people, even if the article were no more than a pin; and I daresay I was ready and willing to perform my part in that pleasing matter.

The day on which I was to visit the tor arrived, but of the earlier part of it I have no recollection. I do, however, distinctly remember passing up across the common, in charge of the good Ann Wilcocks, and making my way to the dark-looking opening that she pointed out to me as the place where the pixies dwelt. I remember climbing over the rocks with which the common at the base of the tor is strewn, and which seemed very formidable barriers to me then, and eventually drawing near to the cave. Then suddenly a little creature darted out from between the masses of granite, and as suddenly disappeared. I felt quite sure it was a pixy, and I was delighted at what I regarded as my good fortune at seeing one. It was just the size that it had been explained to me the pixies were, and vanished, too, in the twinkling of an eye, exactly as I had been taught to expect they would do. Of course, I called to Ann Wilcocks and told her what I had seen. But Ann said she thought it must have been a rabbit. This disappointed me, but was not convincing.

But the most important of the rocky abodes of these little people is the Piskies' Holt in Huccaby Cleave, in which, according to local story, troops of them used to gather. Near it the West Dart flows to meet its sister stream, and we can well imagine that often of a moonlight night the deep gorge through which the united river forces its way was filled with these little people, hastening to their chief gathering place near New Bridge, below the village of Holne. Bounding over the turf, and making light of the rocks in their path, they would press down the valley, being joined here and there by other troops, all anxious to reach the bridge and indulge in their gambols on the beautiful piece of level sward which local story still tells us once formed their *al fresco* ballroom. They would be joined by many from the woods of Brimpts, and further down the stream by others from the combe that descends from near Combestone Tor, in which the quickbeam, or mountain ash flourishes, and which forms a charming haunt for the tiny elves. Still further down they would find their number increased by troops from around the tors that rise above Rowbrook, while already the valley would be filled by those who found in White Wood a congenial place of abode. And so they would press forward, their number growing larger as they progressed, until a bend in the river brought them to their trysting-place.

"A haunt of the pixies", near Combestone Tor.

No spot on Dartmoor is more fitting than this for pixy revels. On one side of a fine piece of turf the Dart runs onward towards Holne Chase; on the other the ground rises steeply to the commons above. All around are hills, many clothed with trees, while others show the bare commons reaching to their crest. By the light of the moon crowds of little beings join in the pixy dance, forming themselves for the most part into large circles. Then having enjoyed themselves to their hearts' content, they seek rest on the mossy banks near by, or, perched upon the sprays of the birch and hazel, and watch the other revellers who have come forward in troops to take their places. And so the merriment continues without cessation, fresh dancers coming forward in endless multitude whenever a ring is broken.

> "The laughing elfins leap to see
> Each other tripping blithesomely,
> Yet pay they, with submissive mien.
> Due homage to their silvery Queen,
> Until her rays cannot be seen:
> Then, conscious that the day is near,
> With silent caution disappear –
> Seek their soft beds in loveliest flowers,
> And sleep away the daylight hours."
>
> (Robert Dyer)

Such were the scenes the old-time peasant believed were to be witnessed on the green near where the Dart takes leave of the wild moor that gave it birth.

It is not our province here to enquire into the origin of the pixy superstition, but only to record some of their doings. Whether they were the souls of unbaptised children, as the peasantry used to say, is a question with which we need not concern ourselves; and why the little elves never show themselves at the present day is another we need not trouble about. Taking a broad view of them it is possible to say that on the whole they appear to be more desirous of helping man than of injuring him. Of course, there are instances where the reverse seems to be the case, but even here it is generally seen that it has been the fault of the person injured. By far the greater number of stories related of them go to show that they are desirous of rendering services to industrious labourers and farmers, but withold their favours, and even inflict some punishment, on those who neglect their work. Pixy-led travellers may probably consider themselves injured when they cannot find their way over the moor; but may it not be that they are merely being drawn away from ground regarded by the pixies as theirs? Such intrusion may have been an unwitting act it is true, but how were the pixies to know that?

To be 'pixy-led' is the one thing most frequently named on Dartmoor in connection with the little elves at the present day, and that this should be so is not surprising. To be overtaken by a mist on Dartmoor is bewildering. Objects appear so distorted that even those that are well known are unrecognisable at a short distance, and endeavours to find the path often proving fruitless it is easy to understand how the influence of some supernatural power is suspected. Those who do not know the moor may, perhaps, be constrained to wander for hours in such circumstances, while even those who are acquainted with it cannot always follow the course they would wish, though they are not likely to wander far from their way unless objects intervene to turn them from it. I remember once when on Skerraton Down, during a thick mist, being totally unable to find a certain point which it was necessary for me to reach, notwithstanding that the ground was known to me. A green path runs across the down, and at a short distance from one end of this, in a hollow through which a rivulet runs down to the Dean Burn, is a hunting-gate. It was the latter that I desired to reach, but I found myself quite unable to do so. On leaving the path I rode on towards the gate as I supposed, but on descending into the hollow could see nothing of it. I used every endeavour to find it, but the mist was so dense that no objects whatever could be recognised, and as I had to ride to Hexworthy and the evening was advancing, I was at length obliged to give up the search. Had I been a stranger to the locality I might have found myself unable to leave the spot, and with a decided right to think I was pixy-led, but as it was I made a cast for the path, and having found it retraced my steps to the lane by which I had entered on the down. My only concern was for my pony, to which my failure to find the way across the hollow meant a longer journey by several miles.

On that part of Dartmoor which seems to have been known in the seventeenth century as Mis Tor Moor is a small mass of granite bearing the name of the Church Rock. By placing the ear against this, it was formerly said, the sound of bells could be heard at certain times, and this was supposed to be caused by the pixies in their retreat beneath the rock. The sounds were likened to those of church bells, and were always to be heard on a Sunday, just before the time for service. It is said that the pixies were fond of bell-ringing, though they do not appear to have been in the habit of doing anything more than climb up the ropes in the belfries of the village churches. Perhaps they preferred more subdued sounds, and accordingly rang only underground. But they do not appear to have been very musical, for it is said that the sound in which they chiefly delighted was the chirping of the cricket.

The sweet bard of the Tavy, William Browne, in his *Britannia's Pastorals*, written some three centuries ago, has left us some charming descriptions of the little people. He has also given us a picture of Indiscombe – or, as he names it – 'Sweet Ina's, Combe', near Tavistock. Through this delightful little valley runs a tributary of the Tavy, called, like several of the Dartmoor streams, the Walla Brook, a name there is little doubt derived from the Wealas, as the native Britons were called by their Saxon conquerors. In this combe the Walla forms at one place a tranquil reach, which, overhung by trees, and margined by mossy banks, forms what is still known as the Pixies' Pool. On its verge the little people were wont to disport themselves when the moonbeams danced upon the water, and woe to the wayfarer who chanced to intrude himself upon their revels. No restful pillow would be his that night. The valley would become a maze, and no shelter would he be able to gain unless he chose to content himself with that provided by the trees in Grammerby Wood. Only when the faint beams of the rising sun stole into the valley would the pixies depart, and not until then would the hapless traveller be freed from their spell.

In these days, when nobody is able to get a sight of the merry little elves, it is only to be expected that there should be some inquiry as to their appearance. As my view of the pixy at Sheeps Tor was a very transient one, I am unable to describe this from my own knowledge, but I have always understood that they are very active little fellows, about the height of a man's knee, and usually dressed in green. This is the description given of them by various farmers, so the stories tell us, who have found them at work in their barn, and by the good wives who have seen them fly up the wide chimney when they have visited a farmhouse to pinch the maid-servants who were reluctant to leave their beds to begin the duties of the day. But they appear to possess the power of changing their forms, for it has been said that they have been seen leaping about on the moor in the shape of small bundles of rags.

There are many other spots on Dartmoor, besides those we have named, which have witnessed the pixy gatherings, while the scenes of their various pranks are met with everywhere. Floating about the deep gorge of the West Ockment are still some memories of the famous pixy,

Jack How, who was able to squeeze himself through the tiniest hole imaginable, and consequently found keyholes very convenient as a means of entering the farmhouses and cottages. Around Hexworthy the story of the pixy who lured the boy Jan Coo to his death below the lonely farm of Rowbrook, and which I heard many years ago from my old friend Richard Cleave, still lingers. Grimjie, of the Webburn Valley, is not often heard of now, but forty years ago people spoke of him. Near Drewsteignton is the Pixies' Parlour, and on the common above Gidleigh is a charming little ferny hollow, which has also been so named. At the head of the far-famed Hound Tor Combe is Holwell, and here, in the summer nights, the little elves have been known to hold their revels on the sward – that is if credence is to be placed in the stories. The farm at Lane End, near the lower part of Tavy Cleave, at one time received much attention from the pixies, but I cannot discover that they have been seen in the locality during recent years. I suppose, like mortals, they sometimes desire a change of scene, and forsake places that they once seemed to delight in, or, it may be that some weightier reason has driven them away. I incline to believe the latter.

Stories are told of a certain magic ointment possessed by the pixies and which enabled those whose eyes were anointed with it to see them. One of this kind, which I heard at Hexworthy, concerned a farmer's wife who lived somewhere between Princetown and Two Bridges, and ended by the good woman becoming blind in one eye. In the following version the story has a happier termination. Becoming by chance possessed of some of this ointment, but being unaware of its exact nature though she had heard something of its magic properties, the woman, out of curiosity, applied some of it to her right eye. Nothing wonderful happened, and she thought no more about it. But a few days later, when at Tavistock market with her butter and eggs, she was surprised to see a little fellow, of anything but prepossessing appearance, jumping about among the stalls, and helping himself to everything that came in his way, while strange to say although he was acting quite openly, nobody took the least notice of him. He would perch upon the edge of a pannier and select some of the finest eggs, or most enticing apples, right under the nose of the owner, who seemed happily oblivious of the fact that the pick of the basket was being taken by a customer who did not trouble himself about paying. Recovering at length from her surprise, the farmer's wife remembered the ointment, and what she had heard of its magic powers, and had no doubt that she beheld a pixy, who, however, was invisible to others. She went forward and spoke to the daring little peculator.

"You'm making purty bold," she said. "What do 'e mean by such goings on?"

The pixy started. "What!" he cried. "Can you see me?"

"See 'e? Ees, I should think I could," returned the woman. "And 'tis a good job too. I'll soon put a stop to your tricks."

"Which eye can you see me with?" demanded the pixy.

The farmer's wife was about to tell him when she recollected herself. He could only want to know for some evil purpose. In her own defence it would be wise to deceive him.

"With the left," she answered.

"Then you'll never see out of it again," cried the pixy, giving the eye indicated a smart slap.

But the slap in the face that he received was smarter still. The pixy's malice was harmless against the eye that had not been anointed, and the woman proved a match for him. He did not visit Tavistock market again.

By the pool on Cripdon Down, and around the Cuckoo Rock, above Dean Combe, the pixies used often to be seen dancing, but no reports ever come to hand now of their appearance at those spots. Around Holne, in the valley of the Erme, on the verge of Walkhampton Common above the church, and near the farm of Hall on Black Down, old tales told of their gatherings, but one would now watch for them there in vain. The beauty-spots remain, but the little elves that lent so romantic an interest to them are flown. Can it be that man's intrusion near the places they had set apart for themselves was the cause of their deserting them? It may be so, for there are instances which seem to point that way. Tales are told of beautiful gardens being deserted by the pixies, when such have, by fresh owners, been turned into vegetable gardens. Roses and lilies they delighted in; onions and turnips did not attract them. But perhaps we should never discover the reason of their leaving us did we try to, and so it is best to leave it as it is, and look upon the elfin race as one of those things that belonged to an older day without concerning ourselves with the reason why they do not appear to favour the present.

If by chance there should be a few stray ones still about, and any of my readers be pixy-led, it may be as well that they should know how to free themselves from the spell. It is a very simple matter. All that is needed is to take off one's coat, turn it inside out, and put it on again. If the scene happens to be the open moor, and it is raining heavily, it will be advisable not to lose time over this. As the moorman says, be dapper.

✳✳✳✳✳

10

Charms and Spells

Among the men who occasionally worked for Farmer Bledge none was more valued than Moses Creber, for not only was he able to turn his hand to anything, but was also very industrious. One day the farmer sent for him and gave him instructions to plough a certain field, telling him that he wished the work begun on the following morning. The field did not belong to the farmer, but to an acquaintance of his who lived at Fardle, a few miles distant, and who was unable to do the work himself in consequence of two of his horses being temporarily unfit.

The next day Moses was early on the field, and, having put the horses he had brought with him to the plough, at once set to work. But, although they pulled their hardest the plough refused to move more than a few feet. It was as though the implement was embedded in rock, and yet the soil did not appear to be different from that of any other field. It must be the plough that was at fault. Having decided that this was so, Moses went to the farm for another.

But the result with this was precisely similar. The plough would move for about a yard, and then become so firmly fixed that the horses were unable to pull it an inch further. After trying a third plough, and with no greater success, he threw up the job and returned to his master.

The farmer heard his story with surprise.

"We will try again, tomorrow, Moses," he said. "I will go over with you."

On the following day Moses again put his horses to the plough, his master looking on.

"Blossom! Violet!" cried Moses to his team.

The animals started, but immediately came to a dead stop. The plough was stuck fast as before.

"There you be, maister," said Moses. "Just as I told 'ee."

The farmer put his hands to the plough himself, and called to the horses.

Blossom and Violet endeavoured to obey the call, but the plough would not move. Then he sent for the farmer, who had only recently taken the place, and explained matters to him. Another effort was made, but to no purpose.

"I see what 'tis," observed Farmer Bledge, after a few minutes' consideration. "This field is under a spell."

"You don't think so, surely," returned his friend.

"It must be so. The plough is all right, and the horses couldn't be better. The fault must be with the field."

At that moment an old labourer came up.

"You daun' main for to say you'm tryin' to plough this field, Farmer Berry," he said. "Way, you'll never do 't. Tisn' possible to break'n. Anybody 'bout heer could ha' told 'e that."

"But what does it mean at all?" asked Farmer Berry.

"The field ban't be crockt I tell you. What it mains I daun't zackly knaw, but I have heerd mun tell that 'twas ordered to be so by some wise man back in old anshent times."

"Wise man," cried Farmer Berry. "I don't see much wisdom in that."

"Well, that's what us call people that can do they sort o' things. I can't tell 'e no more than I've said. You wan't break this field if you try ever so."

" 'Tis as I said," declared Farmer Bledge; "a spell has been cast upon the field. We may as well go home Moses."

And the belief continued down to our own time that the Fardle field could never be broken.

Another story exists of a chamber in a large house on the southern verge of the moor once being under some weird influence, though happily means were eventually found to break the spell. Dreadful things had happened in the room it was said. Those who had slept in it had been rudely awakened during the night, and their heads had been dashed against the four walls by some unseen power. How they survived such treatment the story does not explain, but it is presumed they must have done so, otherwise it is difficult to see how the manner in which they were served should become known. That this could not be allowed to continue it is needless to say, and after some consultation the inmates decided that the best thing they could do was to send for a 'wise man' to 'lay' the spirit which they did not doubt occasioned such a dreadful state of things.

The 'wise man' came, and listened to the story. Then he undertook to break the spell but explained that it would be necessary for him to go to the room alone. This was unfortunate, as it deprives us of learning the means he adopted to effect the desired object. But the fact that the room was freed from the spell is, after all, the one thing that matters, and we must not complain because the 'wise man' did not give the trick away. He would hardly have been a wise man had he done so. Who was the first to put the efforts of the exorcist to the test I cannot say, but he must have been a man of great courage or of great faith.

On the side of the hill on which rise the grey masses of Rippon Tor is a cross cut in relief on the surface of a rock, the only instance of such a thing that occurs on Dartmoor. My friend and fellow-lover of the moor, Mr. C. Spence Bate, has suggested as a reason for this that the spot may once have been in evil repute as under the spell of some malignant power, and that the cross was carved there in order to free it from that baneful influence. Whether he was right in his conjecture or not we know that crosses were sometimes placed on spots of that kind in the belief that such a result would follow, though none other of these objects on Dartmoor seem to require such an explanation of their existence. There is the possible exception of Childe's Tomb. In that case, as my discovery of the monument has shown, a kistvaen, usually regarded as a heathen grave, was surmounted with a cross. If the monks of Tavistock which tradition connects with the tomb, erected this cross it may possibly have been for the reason that they found some legend attaching to the kistvaen which associated it with thought they were anxious to suppress, and considered there could be no better means of doing this than by conferring a sanctity upon the object by setting over it the symbol of the Christian faith. This is possible, but at the same time it may well have been that if the monks did place the cross there it was not alone as a charm to dispel a heathen superstition. The story tells us that they conveyed the body of Childe from the Forest of Dartmoor to Tavistock, and buried it there, and so, by the terms of his testament, received his lands. Such a rich reward would demand some recognition to the testator, and a cenotaph on the moor would prove a suitable acknowledgment, and possess the merit of being inexpensive.

The sign of the cross, as we know, has always been a potent charm against evil. The early saints employed it with wonderful effect, we are told. When St. Frodobert was a little boy a devil used to meet him on his way to school, probably objecting to the spread of education. But the budding saint was easily his match. He simply made the sign of the cross, and saw no more of him. Another saint – Sulpicius – is also said to have resorted to the same charm when a child, scaring by it two devils who haunted a ruined church into which he went to pray at night. Both these instances occurred so far back as the seventh century, but similar ones are related of times much nearer our own, and with quite as much truth.

In the romantic valley of Dean Burn is the Hound's Pool, into which the little river, hurrying down from the moor, falls in a silvery cascade. Here a poor weaver is condemned ceaselessly to toil under a spell cast upon him, not as one might suppose by a wicked witch or sorcerer, but by the parson of the parish. The weaver, whose name was Knowles, does not appear to have done anything deserving of the fate to which the parson condemned him, and is certainly a much injured spirit. Knowles, it appears, was a prosperous man, but as death comes to rich and poor alike, so he knocked one day at his door. He was buried, and, of course, everybody thought that they had seen the last of him. But in this they were mistaken, for, on the following day he was seen to be working at his loom as usual. His son, who if he had been a sensible man, would have been glad to see his father back again and at work, ran off to consult the parson, and brought him to the house. The latter commanded Knowles, who was upstairs, to come down, which the

The Hound's Pool, in the valley of the Dean Burn.

weaver agreed to do when the quill in his shuttle was worked out. But the parson would brook no delay, and telling him that he had been at work long enough, ordered him at once to give over. Knowles obeyed, and the parson, taking a handful of earth that he had brought from the churchyard, threw it in his face, and the spirit of the unfortunate weaver was instantly changed into a black dog. The parson, commanding the animal to follow him, led the way to the valley of Dean Burn, and stopping on the brink of a pool, gave him a nutshell, and told him that when he had dipped the water from it he should be at rest. Such a task anybody would deem to be impossible, but the parson seems to have had his doubts, for he was careful to give the dog a nutshell with a hole in it! The imposition of a task that can never be completed is found in the folk tales of most countries, and as we have seen, figures in several stories connected with Dartmoor, such as that of the emptying of Cranmere by Binjie, the twisting of ropes of sand in the Erme, and the hound which runs from the gate of Fitzford to Okehampton Park to fetch a blade of grass, a journey which must nightly be performed until not a single blade remains.

Associated with these stories of spells we sometimes find others showing how by certain charms the evil may be averted. Thus wicked spirits may be prevented from troubling a man in another world if the precaution be taken of carrying the corpse through running water when on the way to burial. It is not so many years since such a case occurred in the neighbourhood in which I write, and it has always been a popular belief that the pixies have no power over a man if he can succeed in placing a stream between himself and them. In fact 'wishtness', as the Dartmoor man styles all supernatural influences, cannot pursue a dead or a living man across water. This belief, if not as old as the hills, is yet of remote antiquity. As we know in the rites of the cleansing of the leper, described in the book of Leviticus, the bird was to be killed "over the running water". And this transferring of the evil, as it were, is found in many of the charms that are even yet practised by some of the country people; for very often one part of the ceremony consists in casting away the leaf or plant, or other object used in the charm, in the belief that as the latter perishes or decays, so will the trouble pass away.

Tom Rattenbury had for some time cast longing eyes towards Sarah Joyce, and Sarah, with the quick perception of her sex, was fully aware of it. But Tom was naturally diffident, and though opportunities of declaring himself often arose he always failed to seize them. Perhaps this state of matters may have continued had not a possible rival appeared on the scene. This was young Jonas Pawley, who having left his employment near Ashburton, had returned to Widecombe, where Tom and the pretty Sarah Joyce resided. Tom viewed his acquaintanceship with the girl he was himself so fond of with some concern, for he could not but recognise that Jonas was a fine, dashing fellow, and when at length he heard him publicly express his opinion that Sarah was the prettiest maid in the parish, he thought it was time for him to bestir himself.

As a first step he broached the subject to his mother.

"Like to get mar'ied, should 'e," she replied, when Tom had made known his desire. "Ees, I daresay you would; 'tis like most of 'e. But there, I daun' find no fault wi't. You've always been a good b'y, and I wouldn' stand in your way for the worl'. As for Sarah Joyce, nobody can't say nothin' 'gainst she. Ees, I'm agreeable to it if her be."

"I ant said nort eet," explained Tom.

"Ant said nort?" cried his mother. "Then what be talkin' 'bout it for? S'pose you think you can have her for the askin'. That's always the way with the main. Think the maidens be ready to snap up the first wan that com's along. I b'lieve your father thought like that, but I didn' laive 'm get me so aisy."

"But he got 'e though," observed Tom.

"Well, ees, he did arter a bit," admitted Mrs. Rattenbury. "But what could I do when he wouldn' take 'No' for an answer? But you mightn' find Sarah Joyce have so much pity 'pon 'e as I had 'pon your father. But what be gwain to do; be agwain to spaik to her?"

"I'd like to, but I'm most 'shamed to; I'm feared her'll laugh at thacky."

And Tom placed his hand on a large wen on his forehead.

"Ees, to be sure," said his mother; "it daun't improve your handsomeness. I mind your father had wan; never couldn't wear his hat like another man. You ought to ha' done what I've told 'e so many times. Go up and see th' ole man Tarbut, to be sure. He'll soon send 'n away for 'e."

"Think he could?"

"Sure of it. Foo things Dan'l can't do."

"P'raps he could get rids o' my worts, too."

"If you 'low 'un to spaik a foo words auver mun, and do as he tells 'e to, they'll soon go 'way. Take my advise; go up and see Dan'l tomorrow mornin'."

Tom did not fail to do so, and found Daniel Tarbut in his little garden. In a few words he told the old man what he required.

Daniel looked at the wen and then at the warts, and finally expressed his readiness to work a charm that would rid Tom of them completely. Bidding the latter take a seat, he went to the further end of the garden, and plucking a certain herb from the hedge, he speedily returned with it, bringing with him also a small bit of groundsel. Drawing a chair close to Tom he sat down, struck the wen several times, repeating to himself certain words, which he explained were not for Tom to hear. When this was done he placed the herb in Tom's hand and told him to put it in his pocket.

"I've a repaited the proper words," said Mr. Tarbut, looking very wise; "and I daun't think the charm will fail. I knaw he wan't if 'tis a wain you've a got 'pon your haid. You'll find that as the harb withers away in your pocket so the wain'll graw smaller and smaller till you can't see un. If he dithn' us shall knaw 'tisn' a wain, and then it'll be to find out what 'tis."

After delivering himself of this carefully-guarded speech Mr. Tarbut turned to the warts, and went through a similar ceremony with them.

"When you get home," he said, "go in your garden, and take the piece of groundsel I've a struck your worts wi' and thraw it auver your shoulder. You musn' look behind 'e, and you musn' see where't goes, but you must thraw it so as 't'll fall 'pon another man's ground. Then as it rots so your worts'll go 'way. But you must mind that you thraw it right; if you daun't 'twant be no good."

Tom went home, and was careful to obey Mr. Tarbut's injunctions to the letter. But when a week had passed and the herb in his pocket had withered without any effect being produced on the wen, and, although there had been ample time for the groundsel to decay, the warts still adorned his knuckles, he began to have grave doubts about the efficacy of the wise man's charms. But his mother would not hear of this. "Dan'l was a most knowledgable man," she said. "The charm must have time to work."

Tom waited another week, but the wen and the warts were still in evidence. He began to think he should never be in a fit state to present himself before Sarah Joyce, when something happened that decided him to do so in spite of the awkward excrescences. Jonas Pawley had actually walked home from church with her. Tom saw that it was now or never, and lost no time in repairing to her cottage.

He entered and found Sarah alone, but was at a loss how to announce the object of his visit. He talked about Farmer Blewett's turnips; of the new pump at old Sally Brown's; and how the parson's cart had been painted blue; but was unable to utter what he desired. Then, moved by some impulse that he could not control, he actually referred to the very thing he had been anxious to keep out of sight.

"Got a bit of a wen heer," he said lifting his hand awkwardly to his forehead.

Sarah looked at it as though she had never noticed it before.

"Why, bless me, so you have," she said. "But that's nothing. It would soon disappear if you had it charmed."

"I'm glad sure 'nough to hear you say that. I'm sure now it will go. For I've been charmed."

"Who has charmed you?" she asked.

Tom was just about to tell her of his visit to Mr. Tarbut, when a word leapt to his tongue that broke the ice and proved a knock-out blow for Jonas Pawley.

"You," he whispered.

11

Haunted Places and Apparitions

Among the various objects on Dartmoor that speak to us of early times the old tracks that run over its hills and through its valleys are particularly deserving of notice. It is true they present nothing curious or attractive in themselves, and might very well escape the observation of the rambler since vestiges only of them remain, but they none the less possess an interest. This lies in their historical associations. To come upon a path apparently worn by the hoofs of ponies or cattle, and extending only for a short distance, or upon a little fording-place on some stream in a remote part of the forest, may not at first awaken the curiosity of the passer-by, but when he learns that these objects are links in a chain, that they mark the existence of an ancient way from one side of the moor to the other, interest is aroused. Previous to my investigations of these tracks little was known of them; in fact the existence of only a very few had been recorded, but my researches have resulted in showing that Dartmoor is not quite the 'pathless wild' it was once supposed to be. But we are not at present concerned with the antiquarian or historical interest attaching to these tracks but rather to the fancied connection of such old paths in various places with the supernatural, for it is often said that they are haunted. This being so we should, in a district like Dartmoor, naturally expect to find some weird stories clinging to the ancient ways that once crossed it.

But in this the investigator would be disappointed. Such stories are few, and the reason is not far to seek. As the paths gradually became disused so were the legends connected with them forgotten. Possibly there was a time when stories of the knights of Arthur's day, or of the abbots of a later time, were related, and in which the green paths winding through the heather and the solitary ford were made to figure. But the objects being obliterated by time, nothing was left to associate the stories with, and by-and-by they, too, faded from the people's memory. At the same time it is not to be supposed that all are gone. In a few places the path is still shown where, at certain times, the misty form of the cavalier, or fair lady, is seen to walk by the light of the moon.

In the stormy days of the Civil Wars there was at Bovey Tracey a staunch adherent of the king named John Cann, who, when the Parliamentarians triumphed, found himself in danger. To avoid his enemies he abandoned his house, and, taking with him a considerable treasure, sought refuge among the rocks of a tor that rose from the hillside above the town. Here he buried his treasure, and, having found a place of concealment, considered himself safe from pursuit. At night he would venture forth, and pace to and fro upon the sward, but never left the rocks. But it was not for long that he was to remain undisturbed. The Puritans were determined to find him, and, after a while, he was tracked to the tor by bloodhounds. He was conveyed to Exeter and executed, and nothing then remained for his enemies to do but to find the treasure. At first hopes ran high, but after a time a circumstance occurred that put an end to all endeavours to discover it. By the light of the moon John Cann had been seen pacing the short path that his steps had worn on the turf in his days of nature. The ghost of the Royalist was guarding the treasure, and nobody dared to search for it again. It was never found, and though I am not a prophet – I venture to predict that it never will be. But the path may still be seen, and the Royalist's memory is perpetuated by the name of the tor, which is known as John Cann's Rocks.

A part of the road between Ivybridge and Cornwood is known as Houndle Hill, and here a dark lady is sometimes seen to walk. More than one story is related of her, and they are all equally true. One has it that the reason for the lady's walking at this particular spot is that it was here she used to saunter with her lover, from whom cruel fate afterwards separated her. While we may question the wisdom of these visits, since such would only be likely to keep alive saddening thoughts, we cannot but admire the lady's constancy.

By the side of the road leading from Holne to Hexworthy, and not far from Combestone Tor, is a deep hollow extending down the hill towards the Dart. That this hollow was once the scene of the tinners' labours the stone heaps in it plainly show, but so far from defacing it they endow it with an attraction greater than it possessed before. But it is to nature that this is partly due. She has done her work so completely that the stone heaps cast up by the 'old men' of a bygone day have now become moss-clad hillocks on which wave tall ferns, and shelter in the dells between them specimens of the graceful mountain ash, or, as the moor folk call it, the quickbeam. What name this spot bore in former times is not recorded, but that by which it is known now is sadly out of harmony with its natural attractiveness. It is called Hangman's Pit, from the sad circumstance of a man having committed suicide there.

Hangman's Pit, Holne Moor.

Now if this were not an established fact nothing is more certain than that antiquaries would connect the name with the Celtic word 'maen', and tell us that 'hang maen' meant the hanging-stone, and pointed to the fact that a cromlech, or dolmen, once existed there. But it so happens that the event, which occurred in the third decade of the last century, is beyond dispute, and antiquarian speculations are therefore unnecessary. The unfortunate man, who was by occupation a moorman, and lived at Round Hill, near Princetown, hanged himself to one of the trees in the hollow, when on his way home from Brent Fair. It was supported that the rash act was committed in consequence of finding he had made a bad bargain at the fair over the exchange of his pony. This is all that is known of the circumstance, but the story does not end there. At the time when he was supposed to have destroyed himself his wife, who was at their home at Round Hill, saw his shade approaching the door, and it was afterwards reported that this haunted Hangman's Pit. Although I have passed there late at night it has never appeared to me, but a moorman friend of mine once came into Hexworthy and reported that he had seen something very mysterious there. What was it like? was the eager enquiry. He could not describe it very minutely, but said it appeared to him as though white foxes were jumping about in one of the pits. Such animals being, of course, unknown on Dartmoor everybody said he must be mistaken. The moorman could hardly be got to admit that, but finally gave way a little, declaring that if it was not white foxes he had seen it was certainly 'wishtness'.

On the common above Cudlipp Town, beside a grassy path that leads to the forest at Walkham Head, is a low, grassy mound, which was once said to be haunted by the spirit of a suicide whose grave it marks. A young man of the neighbourhood having been deceived by the girl to whom he had given his heart was unable to bear the cruel stroke, and rashly took his life. The poor body was denied Christian burial, and was laid in the earth on the open moor, a stake being driven through it to ensure that it should not rise again. But though this was effectual so far as the body was concerned it could not keep the spirit from rising, and the people in the neighbourhood soon found that it would have been more to their comfort, as it most certainly would have been to their credit, had they caused the body to be decently interred in the churchyard. It was speedily rumoured that the young man's ghost had been seen by the mound, and nobody would pass over the green track after nightfall. How, or when, it was finally laid is unknown, but all in the locality agree in saying that it has never 'walked' within living memory. But the story is not forgotten, and Stephens' Grave may still be seen by the rambler in this part of the moor.

Many a mile lies between this low mound on Cudlipp Town Down and the spot on which another suicide was buried many years ago. The latter is known as Jay's Grave, and is situated by the side of the road skirting the down between Swallaton Gate and a farm called Ford, in the parish of Manaton. What drove Kitty Jay to the act of self-destruction is unknown, but local story has it that she hanged herself in a barn. The barbarous custom of the time decreed that she should be buried by the roadside, and so they laid her in this lonely spot. The little grave still exists, but the shade of the unfortunate girl has long ceased to visit it.

Stories were once current of highwaymen who waylaid travellers on the moor, and of some who were hanged in chains on the scene of their nefarious exploits. According to local report Black Down, a part of Dartmoor lying between Tavistock and Lydford, was once a favourite lurking place with the knights of the road. Suddenly dashing from their place of concealment they would call upon the coachman to stop, and then levy toll upon the passengers; or, in the case of horsemen, command them to "stand and deliver", while covering them with a pistol. Having secured their booty they would put spurs to their horses, and taking to the moor, would soon be beyond pursuit.

But these daring spirits did not always find that their adventures had this happy termination. They sometimes got the worst of it, and then the last act in the drama of their lives took place on the scaffold at Exeter gaol. But although their earthly career was over, more followed. An example was needed to warn others of their fraternity of the fate in store for them if they did not discontinue their evil ways, and so the body was sent down to the place where their last crime was committed, and there suspended from a gibbet until only a ghastly skeleton remained. On Black Down those days – which we are in the habit of referring to as the 'good old times' – commemorated in the name of its most prominent eminence, which is known as Gibbet Hill. There are now no remains of the hideous apparatus to be seen upon it, but there are those living in the parish whose fathers remembered when such existed there.

Of course with such a terrifying object as a dead man swinging from a beam to the accompaniment of the rattling of the chains that secured him uncanny stories would associate. The shade of the dashing highwayman, mounted on a phantom horse, and with pistol in hand, would be seen at the foot of the gibbet as though awaiting the arrival of travellers from whom to extort well-filled purses as in his days of nature. If the exposure of the corpse did not frighten others who pursued a similar trade to that of the executed felon, it is certain that it frightened many an innocent villager, and caused him to shun the spot where the gibbet stood. If compelled to pass it after nightfall he would walk swiftly by, not daring to look about him, starting at the slightest sound, and seeing a ghost in every bush. And thus the spot came to be 'haunted' by the spirit of the bold Colonel Dick or Captain Jack.

Perhaps the most noted of the Dartmoor highwaymen was John Fall, who conducted most of his operations on the road leading moorward from Moretonhampstead. Whether he ultimately graced a gibbet is uncertain, but it is affirmed that one was once erected at Watching Place in the midst of the scene of his labours, and that this was the last instance of such an example being made in this part of the county. The spot is now usually spoken of as Beetor Cross, the name having reference to the cross-roads there and to the farm of Beetor near by. But it also has another meaning for here is to be seen an ancient stone cross, which, after being taken away to serve as a gatepost, was brought back some years ago and set up on, or close to, its original site. I am not aware whether the ghost of a highwayman was ever seen at this place, but I think I shall be safe in affirming that none has visited it since the re-erection of the cross.

Among the buildings in this Dartmoor country to which attach traditions concerning ghostly visitants the most important is Lydford Castle, in which during several centuries the forest courts were held and which was also the Stannary prison. Little now remains of it but the bare walls of the keep, but these prove sufficient shelter for the ghost that is said to haunt the place. This appears in the form of a black pig, and is said to be the shade of the notorious Judge Jeffreys. But there is no evidence that Jeffreys ever presided at the Lydford courts – it is only reported that he did so – and it would, therefore, be unsafe to suppose that the pig has anything to do with him. Besides, it is a libel on that animal to connect Jeffreys with him. A pig is a harmless, inoffensive quadruped, to whom we are indebted for our hams and bacon; the judge was a savage and cruel monster to whom we owe only our scorn and disgust. Every man has a right to his opinion, of course, and there may be those who will disagree with me, but I absolutely refuse to believe that the black pig sometimes seen in the court of Lydford Castle is the ghost of Judge Jeffreys.

Between the Bedford Hotel and the vicarage at Tavistock is an ivy-covered ruin that once formed the gateway leading from the abbey to the gardens belonging to it. It consists of a low arched passage with a tower on each side of it, and local story once had it that the southernmost of these was haunted by the ghost of a woman who was there murdered by a soldier. Her name was Betsy Grimbal, but who or what she was, or the circumstances of the tragedy, tradition does not tell us. Marks on the wall of the narrow stone staircase that led to the top of the tower used to be pointed out as blood-stains, and people shunned the place after nightfall. The story is kept alive by the name of the ruin, or rather of that part of it in which the dark deed was perpetrated, this being known as Betsy Grimbal's Tower.

On the border of the moor at Buckfast was another abbey, and this, too, had its spectre. Long years ago one of the abbey's benefactors was

Sir William Kingdon, and when he died the monks laid him in the abbey church. Twelve months passed away, and the anniversary of his death, the 3rd of July, was solemnly observed by the monks. But in the midst of the service they were struck with sudden fear, for on the spot where their benefactor had been buried there appeared a misty form, which taking shape, revealed the lineaments of Sir William. The service concluded, and the good brothers went silently to their cells. Little was said on the morrow, for they knew not what the strange appearance might portend, and judged it best to be silent. Another twelve months passed, and again the shade of Sir William appeared at the vault in the abbey church. The brothers knew not what to do, and, like wise men, did nothing. But ever after the ghost appeared on the anniversary of the day on which Sir William died. Time passed on:–

"Bluff Harry broke into the spence
And sent the cowls adrift,"

but he could not drive away the ghost, for even when the abbey became a ruin it continued to haunt the knight's place of burial.

An ancient manor house on the border of the moor is haunted by a spirit known as the White Lady, and a solitary farmhouse at Lane End, in the vicinity of Tavy Cleave, was at one time visited by the shade of its former occupier. Not very far from the latter, but on the other side of the Tavy, is the farm of Stannon, and this, too, was once the scene of 'wishtness'. In this instance, however, the ghost was never seen, but the effect of its visits was none the less uncomfortably apparent. It seemed to delight in scattering the furniture about the place. The kitchen table would be found upside down; chairs that belonged in the parlour would be found in the bedroom; while the beds were often carried to the wash-house, and the grandfather clock laid on its face in the passage. Near the church at Brent is a house at one time belonging to a farm, and in my boyhood days it used to be told how it was haunted by the ghost of a man who had committed suicide there. But all these spectral visitations have ceased, and if a labourer with whom I was once speaking on these matters was correct, the reason is simple.

"People can't come back now," he said, "not if they wanted to ever so. They've never been able to since the parsons made some alteration in the burial service."

❋❋❋❋❋

12

Works of the Weird Sisters

In my remarks on charms and spells I have spoken of certain people and places said to have been under magic influences; I now propose to give some account of those who were formerly believed to possess the power to cause these evils. From the earliest times there has existed a belief in witchcraft, both among civilised peoples and among savage tribes. In the days of Moses witchcraft and divination were practised; those who had familiar spirits were to be avoided and it was commanded that a witch should be put to death. Saul visited the Witch of Endor; the prophet Micah utters a warning against witchcraft, as also did Paul. In every age we find references to the practisers of the black art and they have been consulted by high and low down to our own day; from the Thane of Glamis to the untutored peasant.

We usually regard a witch as being an old woman, but in Devonshire the term is sometimes also applied to a man who professes to be skilled in the kind of necromancy believed in by the country people, the word wizard never being used. Thus the White Witch who lived near the borders of the moor not many years ago was a man, and was credited with being exceedingly clever. It is only fair to state that he was chiefly sought after by those who imagined themselves to be bewitched by somebody else, in order to counteract the spell that had been cast over them, and not for the purpose of acting as an agent to injure others. In spite of the title by which he was known, he appears to have been more like a 'wise man' than a wizard, though probably he claimed the power that is supposed to belong to the latter. But the true witch, the ancient beldame of the stories, seldom sought to do good. She may occasionally, when her interests demanded it (for pecuniary considerations weigh even with witches) have assumed the part of the 'wise woman', and muttered charms warranted to heal some wound or scald; but her chief delight was to blight the life of some poor victim on whom she had cast her evil eye. It was in her power to do this that she prided herself; a power which at first assumed she came at length to believe to be real.

At the present day the witch is suffered to weave her spells just as she pleases, nobody being the better or the worse for what she does, but our ancestors were not so lenient. They believed in her power to work evil, and acted up to the Levitical injunction when such was proved against her. And often, it is to be feared in cases in which the accused was innocent of any pretence to magic power. The witch-finder had to justify his existence, and when he made charges he generally contrived that evidence in support of them should be forthcoming. On the other hand, there are numerous instances where women accused of the crime of witchcraft have admitted the charges to be true, gratified, it is supposed, with being believed to possess magic power. Such, it seems probable, was the case with the three women who were tried at Exeter in 1682.

These women, Temperance Lloyd, Mary Trembles, and Susanna Edwards, practised their art, or pretended to, in the north of Devon, and a charge of witchcraft being preferred against them, they were brought before the magistrates at Bideford and committed. Being found guilty at Exeter, they were condemned to be hanged, and the sentence was duly carried out. They confessed that they had done much mischief, stating among other things that they had squeezed one Hannah Thomas to death in their arms. They also said that through their means several ships had been cast away, and that they had caused a boy to fall from the top of a main mast into the sea. Their confessions were taken before Thomas Gist, Mayor of Bideford, and John Davie, alderman of that town. Of the wisdom of these worthy men a great deal might be said, but as this will be apparent to the reader it is unnecessary for me to further remark upon it.

The earliest of the witches of Dartmoor lives only in fiction, and not in the traditions of the people. She is introduced in a poem by the Rev. John Johns, the author of the *Dews of Castalie*, which was published in 1828. A story exists in the forest that Piers Gaveston, during one of his banishments from Court, sought concealment on Dartmoor. In the poem *The Witch of Sheeps Tor* finds Gaveston at Crazy Well Pool, and in a cryptic manner reveals his fate. But the tradition says nothing of this; it merely tells us that the favourite once found shelter on the moor, and probably had its origin in the fact that in 1307 Edward II granted the forest to Gaveston. At the latter's death it reverted to the Crown. But if Mr. Johns has given us only an imaginary witch he has at all events rendered us his debtors by contributing to the literature of Dartmoor one of the finest poems that its wild hills have ever inspired.

Among the powers formerly attributed to witches was that of transforming themselves into some animal. The ogre in the story of *Puss in Boots* possessed it, much to his cost, and instances of it occur in the stories in the *Arabian Nights*. Several are found on Dartmoor, most of them naming a hare as being a favourite animal with these weird workers of charms. One tells us how an old witch, who lived somewhere in the neighbourhood of the charming little village of Buckland-in-the-Moor was in the habit of changing herself into a hare in order to gain the shilling which the master of the harriers was always ready to give to anyone who could tell him where puss could be found.

Cottages at Buckland.

Her agent in this matter was her little grandson, who, whenever the harriers met in the neighbourhood, was sure to be present, and able to inform the master that "he knew by a hare". It always turned out that the boy was right. He would lead the field to some spot near by, and there, sure enough, a hare would be found, and the boy would be rewarded accordingly. But after a time it was noticed by the huntsman that although they could depend upon the boy showing them a hare they never succeeded in killing it. This seemed very strange, and the huntsman determined that on the next occasion he would give the hare no chance. The boy took them to a clover field, and up jumped puss. The harriers were after her like lightning and rapidly gained upon her. Suddenly the boy, forgetting himself in his fear that the hare would be run into, uttered a warning shout.

"Run, Granny, run!" he cried.

This was heard by the huntsman, who dashing forward at his topmost speed, reached the hare just as the foremost hound fixed his teeth into her. The hare freed herself, and turning into an open gate, darted under the door of a cottage.

The huntsman threw himself from his horse, and knocked loudly.

There was no response, and after a similar result following a second summons he flung the door open.

On entering he found an old crone seated on a stool near the hearth dressing a wound in one of her legs that appeared to have been recently inflicted.

Variants of the story tell us that no hounds can ever come up with the witch transformed into a hare, and that nothing but a charmed bullet will have any effect upon her. This, I venture to think, we may safely believe.

A dreaded power of the witch was that of the evil eye. Many stories are related of victims to this malignant glance, which was accompanied by some wish on the part of the sorceress, not however audibly expressed, that ill-fortune should overtake the person on which it rested. Speedily would the power be felt. The poor victim would fall ill, and be unable to take food. Sleep was denied him; and he was racked by constant pains. He knew, and his neighbours knew, that he was 'ill-wished', and that he would never recover unless a counter charm could be discovered. Then old Betsy Jane would be consulted, and some kind of penance would be imposed, and a pecuniary sacrifice ordered to be made, silver being required, to complete the charm. This sometimes proved effective so great was the faith placed in the 'wise woman', but when it did not it often went very hard with the sufferer if he neglected to obtain medical advice. I remember a case that occurred a few years ago, in which a young man sustained a severe cut, which bled profusely. Recourse was at once had to a 'wise man', who came and 'said a few words' over the wounded limb, in the hope of checking the flow of blood. But this had no effect, and the young man was removed to the hospital at Tavistock. He arrived there just in time; any further delay, it was said, might have proved fatal.

And the witch's power was exercised over animals also. Sometimes a cow would pine away in spite of the best of feeding, or a horse would become unaccountably lame. Instead of sending for a veterinary surgeon, the peasant of an older day would often persuade himself that his misfortunes arose from his being 'ill-wished', and thought of no other remedy but the charm that old Betsy was supposed to be able to work in such cases. If the animal recovered, of course the 'wise woman' earned the credit of it; if it did not, the unfortunate result was declared to be owing to the 'ill wisher' having been first in the field.

The use of the knotted cord, which was a common practice in early times, in various parts of the world, was not unknown to the witch of the countryside. When it was designed to inflict some injury upon a person the witch would tie a number of knots in a cord, and over the first one would utter some charm, at the same time blowing upon it. Then the victim would begin to feel the ill-effects of the enchantment. On the following day the charm would be repeated over the second knot, and the victim would grow worse. This went on until the last knot was reached, when the illness would either prove fatal – or the victim would recover, the witch being ready with an explanation in either case. There is a story of a Jew who bewitched Mohammed, by tying eleven knots in a cord. It was hidden in a well, but this being revealed to the prophet he sent for it, and having repeated over it two chapters of the Koran, was freed from the charm. These two chapters refer to charms, in one of them the request being made for deliverance from "the mischief of women blowing on knots".

One of the best known among those who claimed to possess the power of weaving spells was Bet Webb, who was known as the witch of Dartmoor. She lived at Post Bridge and many stories of her wondrous achievements used to be related in the district. On one occasion the driver of a carriage, who was taking a small party to Widecombe, incurred her displeasure by some means, and the evil eye was at once turned upon him. Being the opposite of superstitious he thought nothing of this, nor of the prophecy that he would meet with trouble before the end of his journey was reached, and, as he told me, soon forgot all about it. But when near Runnage, and not far on his road, he was suddenly reminded of her words. An effectual stop was put to the journey – at all events for some time – by one of the wheels of the carriage coming off.

Tom Upcott was a small farmer in Walkhampton parish, and lived in a solitary house with his wife and two sons. One morning, as he was about to set out to Tavistock market with two young bullocks which he had reared, his wife came into the yard.

"Tummas," she said, giving him a folded paper, "I want you to get me a foo things to Tavistock so I've asked Amos to put um down on this heer paper, and he's done it. You wouln' mind um if I was to tell 'e, so I thought twas best for 'n to write um out wan by wan."

"To be sure," replied Tom, "that's the way. S'pose I can get somebody to raid mun. You know I bant no skollard."

"Way, for sartin' you will in there to Tavistock. Anybody'll raid it for 'e."

Tom put the paper in his pocket, and set off with his cattle.

He had not proceeded far when, at a bend in the road, his horse, startled at the approach of someone, suddenly swerved, and very nearly ran into the newcomer. Tom recognised her as old Mary Mallop, who lived near by, and who was reported to have had dealings in the black art.

"I'm mortal sorry, Mary," he said, pulling up. "This is a young hoss, an' I couldn' help of it."

But the old woman, who was much frightened, grew very angry.

"That's the way you ride 'bout 'pon the roads, be it?" she cried. "You've no care for a body like me, I s'pose. But I wan't be upset for nothin'. You'll suffer for what you've a din; now mark my words, Farmer Upcott."

Tom tried to assure her of his regret for the occurrence, but the old woman would not listen to him, but continued on her way.

"I haup her wan't ill-wish me," said Tom. "Her's a spiteful ole toad, so they say, an' I'm vexed to think I've crossed her."

Arriving at Walkhampton, Tom dismounted and entered the inn. The weather was hot, and he felt thirsty.

Finding an acquaintance within he sat down with him, and in the course of conversation pulled out the paper that his wife had given him.

"Will 'e plaize to raid thacky to me, William?" he said. "Mother gived it to me; 'tis summat for me to carr' home."

His friend took the paper, and after looking at it for a minute or two with a puzzled air announced his ability to decipher the writing.

"Six pennard o' green vardy," he said, reading very slowly. "That's the fust thing."

"Ees, sure," commented Farmer Tom. "Of course us always kaip some o' thacky in th' house. Fine thing for strikin' bruises, an' sich like. Well I can mind that. What be the next thing?"

"Wan poun' an' a-half o' hay."

"What!" cried Tom.

"I main tay. Wan poun' an' a-half o' tay to Mr. Gormet's."

"Ees, ees. Can't do without it."

"Six pennard o' gin," continued William.

"Whats the good o' six pennard?" interrupted Tom.

"Aw, bless 'e, I'm wrong. 'Tis six pennard o' ginger, an' a quart o' vinegar, two poun's o' currants, an' an ounce of allspice."

"I can't abide that ole trade," remarked Tom, "but mother says her likes to put it in cake. Anything futher?"

"Ees," answered his friend. "That bant all of it."

"My basket 'll be purty heavy if there's much more, for I want to carr' home a foo things for my awn use. There's half a gallon o' gin for wan thing – finest med'cine in the worl' for cattle."

"Tis good for everybody," declared William. And then he went on reading.

"Six pound's o' dry fish, an' six poun's o' sugar; quarter poun' o' bakin' powder, and wan poun' o' biscuits – plain wans – I like they that Mr. Peathyjohns sells best. Be sure you get the fish to Mr. Bryant's, the last us had from ole Creely, an' they wudden no thicker than a bit o' paper. That's all," said William; "but what's her put down all thacky nonsense for?"

"I reckon 't's what her said to Amos when she tell' d'n what her wanted me to fetch" explained Tom. "An' the b'y's put down everything her said. But 'tis all right" he continued; "I can mind most o' that, an' what I can't I'll ax somebody to raid to me."

When Farmer Tom issued from the inn a little later he was surprised to find that his bullocks, which he had left in charge of a boy, were nowhere to be seen. He had not brought his dog with him, the animal having injured its leg.

"Where's the bullocks, b'y?" he shouted to the young urchin, who was playing with some companions near by.

The boy looked round, and for the first time became aware that the animals had disappeared.

"Gone up the lane I reckon," he answered. "Can't be far, Farmer Upcott."

Tom mounted his pony and set off, but failed to see anything of his bullocks. Then he returned and tried in another direction, but with no better result. At the end of an hour he was still without them, and feeling hot and angry. Then he suddenly remembered his encounter with Mary Mallop.

"That's of it," he said. " 'Tis th' ole woman's work. I'm bewitched for sartin."

He reflected for a few moments. Of what use was it for him to go to Tavistock now? His bullocks would soon be in the pound, and he could do no business. But what about the commissions with which he was charged? It would never do to return empty-handed.

Accordingly he took his way to Tavistock, vexed at his ill-luck, and in no mood to join the acquaintances he was in the habit of meeting there. When about to enter Mr. Gormet's shop he put his hand in his pocket for the paper his wife had given him. It was not there.

"Dass 'e!" he exclaimed. "If I have'n a bin an' laive'n to Walkhamp'm. I must do the best I can without 'n."

He did; and having filled his basket set out for home. One thing annoyed him particularly. A dealer who had seen his bullocks a few days before came to him and offered him a price for them, fully two pounds more than he had expected to get, but as it was required that they should be delivered at once in order to be sent away with others that the dealer had bought, the bargain could not be struck.

On arriving home he set his basket upon the table, and his wife began to unpack it as usual.

"My gracious, father!" she cried, after having taken out two or three of the articles. "Whatever have 'e got heer? Enough green vardy to last for a hunderd yeers."

Tom looked at her helplessly.

"I'm bewitched," he said.

"Daun't talk sich nonsense to me. You've been drinkin', I b'lieve."

" 'Tis ole Mary Mallop's work," declared Tom. "Aw dear; her's ill-wished me."

"My days!" cried Mrs. Upcott, holding up a tiny parcel; "and this is the tay I wanted, is it. Way there bant no more'n enough for wance or twice. You good-for-nothin' fella, what have 'e been about? Look heer. Heer's enough ginger to fill a bucket. Call that two pounds o' currants, do 'e. An' where's the allspice."

"I forgot it," replied Tom, meekly.

"Forgot it! You didn' forget the gin I'll warn. No, heer 'tis. Mind yourself, daun't 'e."

"I'm bewitched, I tell 'e."

"I'll bewitch 'e. I'll tell 'e about it. No vinegar, no dry fish, more bakin' powder than I should want if I lived seven yeers o' Sundays, and enough biscuits to feed the parish. What soart of a price did 'e make of the bullocks?"

"I've a lost mun," replied Tom.

"Lost mun!" cried Mrs. Upcott, holding up her hands in amazement. "Way, whatever do 'e main?"

"I'm bewitched. Everything's gone wrong. 'Tis that ole Mary. Her've a auver-looked me."

At that moment Amos entered the kitchen, attracted by the sight of the things on the table. He took up a small packet that lay among them.

"What do 'e call this?" he asked.

" 'Tis swaitstuff," answered his father. "Mr. Gormet gived it to me. He cal'd it a surprise packet, and said there was a suv-run in some o' mun, an' might be in thacky."

"Us'll soon see that," said Amos, opening the package.

A cry of delight escaped him.

" 'Tis true, father, "Heer he be right enough," he exclaimed, holding up the coin.

There was a knock at the door. It was the dealer whom he had seen at Tavistock.

"I'm going on to Princes Town," he said, "so I thought I'd call in and tell you that I've got an extension of time for delivering my little lot, and if you're in the mind for selling the bullocks I'm open to buy. You know what I offered you this morning."

Tom hesitated. He did not know where his cattle were, but was reluctant to say so. The dealer took it that he was disinclined to sell.

"Now, come on," he said; "let's make a deal. I'll spring two pounds on my offer; that's good money. Say the word and here's the cash. I can have the cattle as I go back. I see they're on the common just below the lower newtake."

The bargain was struck and when the dealer had gone Tom turned to his wife.

"There, mother," he said: "what's think o' thacky? 'Tis all right now, bant it? I've made four poun' more o' the bullocks than I thought to this morning, an' us have got wan poun' out o' the swaitstuff; five pound' clain off. So now us can very well put up wi too much ginger an' not enough tay. Drat that ole Mary Mallop! I'll never believe in witchcraft no more."

❈❈❈❈❈

13

Omens for Good or Ill?

When the famous Devon navigator, Sir Humphrey Gilbert, was compelled to return from Newfoundland without having accomplished his purpose of planting a colony there, he was only rendered the more determined to effect his object. Consequently he made a second attempt, and in this he was successful in completing his design. But on the homeward voyage his vessel foundered, and, according to an old writer, this unfortunate event was preceded by a most strange circumstance. On the 20th August, 1583, Sir Humphrey left St. John's in a small sloop called *The Squirrel*, accompanied by *The Delight* and *The Golden Hind*, with the intention of making some explorations. On the 29th August a sudden storm arose, and *The Delight* was lost, only twelve men being saved out of her company of one hundred. It was now resolved to return to England, and the officers of *The Golden Hind* endeavoured to persuade Sir Humphrey to make the voyage in that vessel, which was much larger than *The Squirrel*. But he refused, saying he would never desert the ship and the crew with whom he had encountered so many dangers. After they had passed the Azores the little vessel was overtaken by a tempest, and the gallant explorer, with all on board, was lost. The old writer to whom we have referred is Risdon, and he tells us that just before the storm arose a very large lion was seen to glide between the ship and the land. The animal, with open jaws, made its way towards *The Golden Hind*, roaring in a fearful manner, and when it had passed the storm broke. Sir Humphrey, with a book in his hand, endeavoured to cheer his men. "Courage, my lads!" he cried; "we are as near to heaven here at sea as on land." This he was heard to repeat several times. At midnight the ship went down.

Those who could believe this story to be true would naturally see in the strange sight that met the eyes of the mariners an omen of impending evil, and would have been equally right with those who in our day see ill-luck in the appearance of a magpie, in the washing of clothes on New Year's Day, or in making one of a party of thirteen. In every age have there been believers in these portents of evil, so that when the Dartmoor man hears the 'cry' of Dart at a distance greater than is usual, or listens to the call of the Brad Stones below Mil Tor, and imagines these sounds to be a foreboding of ill, he is not showing himself different from the man who deems it unlucky to upset the salt or to walk under a ladder.

Not very far from the foot of Cosdon, the huge hill that fills the north-eastern corner of Dartmoor, is the delightful village of South Tawton, and beyond this is Oxenham. The present building takes the place of a more ancient one, and with the family that once dwelt there a curious tradition is connected. It used to be said that when the head of the family was about to die, a white bird, or a bird with a white breast, would be seen hovering near him, and that it might also appear when other members were about to pass away. There is a tract in existence which gives some account of this, and which was printed in 1611. It is entitled *A True Relation of an Apparition in the likeness of a Bird with a white breast, that appeared hovering over the Death Beds of some of the Children of Mr. James Oxenham, of Sale Monachorum, Devon, Gent. Confirmed by sundry witnesses as followeth in the ensuing Treatise.* The branch of the family, it may be explained, which was thus visited by the bird, lived at Zeal Monachorum.

In the *Familiar Letters* of James Howell, an inscription which he saw on a marble monument in a stonecutter's shop in London is given. This set forth several instances of the bird's appearance, and the date of it was 1632. He also states that the stone was to be sent to a place near Exeter, where the strange events happened. Several instances of this omen have been noted since that time, the latest being in 1873.

The tradition is commemorated in a ballad, which tells us that long ago there dwelt in the ancient mansion near the Taw Sir James Oxenham and his only daughter Margaret. To say that she was beautiful would be needless; she is the heroine of the story, and heroines are always supposed to be so. But she was something more. She was a loving child, amiable, generous, and kindly of heart. Of course her hand was sought by more than one, and equally, as a matter of course, the suitor who was not favoured swore to have his revenge. Love affairs always ran on those lines in the old romantic days. In these times the rejected one takes things more philosophically. When he finds he is not wanted he turns his attention to some other quarter where he hopes he will be. But the would-be lover of Margaret Oxenham acted in the

Oxenham, South Tawton.

approved style of his age, and resolved that if he could not have her himself nobody else should. Time passed, and Christmas Eve arrived. The tables were spread in Oxenham Hall, for Sir James was giving a great feast in honour of his daughter, who was to be married on the following day. A gallant company was gathered at the board, but though youth and beauty were everywhere to be seen, none could surpass the charming Margaret, and none were happier than she and the youth who was to possess her hand.

Sir James rose from his seat. His feelings we can well imagine when he looked upon his beautiful daughter and her lover. He could not confine them to his breast. He must give them vent, and he felt he could only do this by making a speech. This is often the case today.

Precisely what he said is not recorded, but we can well imagine how he spoke of his darling child, and told of his grief at parting from her, but yet a grief not so great as the joy he felt at knowing she had given herself to one who would always love and cherish her, and whom she loved in return. He spoke of the youth as his son. And then his feelings seemed to overpower him, and he sank back upon his seat.

But it was not his feelings alone that had an effect upon Sir James. Unnoticed by the guests, but seen only too plainly by the old knight, a white-breasted bird had suddenly appeared. It flew over the festive throng, and Sir James knew what it portended.

The morrow came, and the wedding guests were gathered in South Tawton Church. Merrily rang the bells as the fair Margaret and her lover walked over the flower-strewn pathway to the church. They took their places at the altar, and the priest began the service. But he had uttered only a few words when a man sprang forward, and raising a dagger plunged it into the breast of Margaret, and instantly withdrawing the weapon stabbed himself to the heart. It was the rejected suitor who had thus stolen the bride from his rival. As Margaret closed her eyes in death the white-breasted bird was seen hovering over her.

Another story tells us of a William Oxenham, to whom the bird appeared in 1743. But he was evidently not of the superstitious sort, and though optical proof left him no room for scepticism about the bird itself he obstinately refused to believe that its appearance was an omen of evil. He was not sick enough to die, he said, and in his person it would be proved that what was reported of the bird was nothing but an idle tradition. But he was wrong, for a very little time elapsed before death claimed him.

What has become of the marble monument seen by Howell is not known. It is not at South Tawton nor at Zeal Monachorum, nor is it recorded that any have seen it elsewhere. But that the white-breasted visitant is not a mere phantom seems to have been vouched for, and it has even proved a bird of ill-omen.

From the Taw we pass over the brown ridges of the moor to another river. Daylight was fading, and the heath lay dark and gloomy, when a moorman on his homeward way suddenly drew rein near the rugged pile of Mil Tor that overlooks the gorge of the Dart. A sound had fallen upon his ear, and he listened intently.

The sound was repeated. It came from the river far down below.

"I thought I wud'n wrong," he said. "'Tis the cry o' the Brad Stones. I've heeard it too often not to awn it. Us shall have it a bit roughish for sartin."

He looked at the sky, which was now rapidly darkening, then again gave his pony the rein.

"It daun't look so bad now," he said, as he jogged slowly onward, "but it'll com' for all that. The Brad Stones have never been known to tell wrong. Foul weather be sure to follow their cry. Aye, an wuss than that I fear. I've a noticed it; I've a noticed it. Us shall heer tell o' some misfortune 'fore I'm much older. Wish I didn' think so. But theer; what I knaw, I knaw, an' tidn' in no man's power to change it."

No storm arose that night, but the wizard hand of winter was laid upon the waste, and when the moorman looked out from his little chamber-window in the morning he saw the grass and heather powdered with frost. A brook ran near his dwelling, and its murmuring was usually the first sound that fell upon his ear. But it was silent now; its tiny cascades had been transformed into gleaming ice, and an unwonted stillness rested upon all. The moorman looked up into the clear sky and at the sun peeping above the whitened ridge that rose toward the east. It was a fair scene, but he shook his head.

"Bootivul," he exclaimed. "Bootivul, sure 'nough. But 'twan't last, I never knawed the Brad Stones wrong eet."

It was the Sabbath and away beyond the hill the sun was gilding the tower of Widecombe Church. Among the worshippers were two boys who lived at Runnage, a farm on the border of the forest, a few miles distant. They remained in the village until the evening, and then took their way home. That night it was found that some sheep had strayed, and as it was too late to search for them then, it was arranged that the two lads should look for them in the morning.

They had not long left the house before snowflakes began to dot the heath, and ere long it was completely whitened. But the boys were not to be daunted. They continued their search while the snow grew deeper and deeper. Their efforts met with no success; nothing was to be seen of the sheep and at length it became evident that they would have to return without them. But the thickly falling snow hid every landmark from their view, and they could not be certain of the direction in which their home lay.

By-and-by their strength became exhausted, and their steps, which had gradually grown slower, were altogether stayed. They sank down upon the snow and fell into a deep sleep.

The inmates of the farm, becoming alarmed at their long absence, set out in search of them, and at length discovered them in a hollow that stretched away to the Dart. The sleep of one had become the sleep of death; the other was saved.

The sad news was soon known to the few dwellers in the locality. It reached the house of the moorman, who heard the story in silence, breaking it only when the recital was done.

"Never knawed mun wrong," he said. " 'Tis sartin as shall heer tell o' some misfortune when the Brad Stones cry."

Tom Babbage lived near Dartmeet, and when he was not to be seen in the immediate locality of that place it was quite certain that he might be found at Pound's Gate. The attraction was the pretty Rosa Creaber, and no lover could be more fond of the girl of his heart than Tom was of her. But beauty is only skin deep, and had Tom known that Rosa had little else but that to recommend her he might have been inclined to doubt whether he was really the fortunate fellow he was supposed to be.

One evening as he made his way over the common to pay his accustomed visit to her, a sound was borne upon the breeze from the deep valley through which the Dart forced its turbulent way.

"Bad weather comin' if 'tis true what they say about the Brad Stones," he remarked. "Don't knaw whether theer's much in the old tale. They do say 'tis a sign of some misfortune, too, but I can't exactly believe that."

When he reached Pound's Gate he found that Rosa had gone out.

"How's that?" asked Tom of her mother when he had learnt the disappointing fact.

"Don't ask me," returned Mrs. Creaber. "I won't have nothing to say about it. You knaw how maidens be."

"What is it you mean?" asked Tom in a tone that betrayed the anxiety he felt. "Where's Rosa gone?"

"Gone out with Jack Barrett, over there to Buckland."

"Jack Barrett!" cried Tom. "What's do 'e mean by that?"

"What I say," replied Mrs. Creaber. "Jack's a been this way purty much lately, and somehow or other it seems to be that the maid's a bit took up weth 'n."

"But we ant had no quarrel," said Tom. "Surely her won't serve me like that."

"I'll have nothing to say. You must ask the maid yourself what her means by it."

"I'll ask Jack Barrett what he means by it," cried Tom. "Only let me catch him."

"Jack means the same as you have all along, I s'pose," replied Mrs. Creaber with an air of indifference, "and if Rosa cares to a gout weth 'n, that's nobody's business but her own. Her'll do as her pleases."

Tom was astounded. Mrs. Creaber had always appeared to be pleased with the attentions he had shown her daughter, and this sudden change of front was so inexplicable that he could hardly believe his ears. He was cut to the heart, too, for he was really fond of Rosa. For a few moments he knew not what to say or do. Then he turned towards the door.

"I'll have a reckoning with Jack Barrett," he said, halting on the threshold; that's a sure thing, and then I'll heer what Rosa's got to say. I hope I shan't meet them tonight, because – "

He stopped. Then abruptly wishing Mrs. Creaber good night, he hurried away.

People saw him pass through the little village, but he seemed to recognise nobody. His brain was in a whirl, and it was some time before he could collect his thoughts. He hardly knew which road he took, but when he became calmer he found that he had reached the commons.

He had walked rapidly, and was glad to slacken his pace. He smiled bitterly as he looked upon the well-known objects around him, and reflected how when he had passed them but a short time before he was filled with happiness at the thought of meeting the girl he loved. Now all was dark. She had slighted him, and the future appeared hopeless. Just then a distant sound rose from the unseen valley near by.

"There's the Brad Stones," he said. "What they tell 'pears true enough now. I never thought much about it before, but – well, theer, I'm 'bliged to since it's come to this. 'Twas always the old people's tale, and it's turned out to be a true wan."

It was some time before Tom Babbage became himself again, but having 'taken it out' of Jack Barrett, and finding that Rosa desired to be off with the old love, he gradually became more resigned. One thing comforted him. It was the coviction he had that Rosa had not preferred Barrett for his own sake, but for what he was likely to bring her. It speedily became known that an old uncle of his who had lately returned from Australia had made Jack his heir, and as he was a very old man there were reasonable prospects of Jack soon enjoying the property. Tom had a little conceit, and would have felt the blow much more had he thought any girl would prefer Jack Barrett to himself.

" 'Twas the money," he said. "Jack's a stupid clout, and Rosa knows it."

She did, but she married him, nevertheless. The presence of the old uncle at the wedding was noted by everybody, and it was agreed that Rosa was a lucky girl.

But in less than six months matters underwent a change, and the future lost its brightness. The uncle took it into his head to follow the nephew's example, and linked himself with a 'widow woman' of Ashburton, who took good care before parting with herself to see that the old man endowed her with all his worldly goods. Jack Barrett bore this reverse with a good heart, but Rosa grew sour and discontented. She neglected the house, and notwithstanding Jack's efforts to make things comfortable, it became a wretched home.

Tom Babbage once more heard the cry of the Brad Stones as he walked over the common, and stopped to listen to it.

"I didn' believe what folks say about they until that night," he said, "and then it com'd home to me plain 'nough. Some might say though that they wudn' right, for 'twas no misfortune for me to be rid of a girl like her who was ready to break her word for a bit of money. But the Stones was right for all that, only their cry was heered by the wrong man."

14

Old People and Old Places

Although the Forest of Dartmoor was once royal demesne, and has, since the time it ceased to be so in 1240, been a possession of the Earls, and, later, of the Dukes of Cornwall, there are nevertheless certain farms within its confines which do not belong to its lord. When, or in what circumstances these enclosures were made, is, of course, not known, but that they are of great antiquity is certain. Their owners hold them by copy of Court Roll, and they are known as the Forest Tenements. Formerly these were thirty-five in number, but during recent years the Duchy have purchased several of them. On some of the commons surrounding the forest there are also farms probably quite as ancient as the tenements themselves, and these together form the oldest habitations on Dartmoor. Besides the preceding there are other houses on the moor, which, if they cannot lay claim to great antiquity, are yet sufficiently old to be interesting. To many of these moorland dwellings a story is found attaching, though it does not usually take us far back into the past. There are, however, references in various records to these Dartmoor farms and other buildings, the dates of which show them to have been in existence at an early period.

The most important of the buildings connected with Dartmoor is Lydford Castle, which we find to have been in a ruinous condition over six hundred years ago. It is so referred to in an Inquisition taken after the death of Edmund, Earl of Cornwall, in 1300, and it is stated that the money received from it did "not suffice to its sustentation". A mill is also spoken of as being situated at Lydford at that time, and this appears to have been a more desirable property than the castle, since it is set down as being worth 26s. 6d a year. The same inquisition mentions a mill in the forest which was even of greater value, for that is said to have produced forty shillings a year.

Just within the forest on its south-eastern border are the two small groups of Forest Tenements named Babeny and Pizwell, the inhabitants of which were permitted by the Bishop of Exeter in 1260 to pay their tithes to the parson of Widecombe, and it was at that church that they attended, their own parish church of Lydford being so far distant. Sherburton, a tenement on the West Dart, is mentioned in 1301, and a little later Dunnabridge, Hexworthy, Brimps, and others. There is also mention of farms on the border commons as Downton, Southerly, and Ouldsbroom in 1344, and, in 1609, of Fernworthy, on the South Teign. "Certayne howses" are also referred to in the latter year as having been erected on Walkhampton Common by the ancestors of Gameliel Slanning, although that extensive waste was at that time claimed as "parcell of the Dutchie of Cornwall". Over the doorway of many of the border farmhouses a date is carved, and sometimes this is seen on those on the moor itself, though the latter is not usual. As these dates do not show a greater age than between two and three hundred years, it is probable that in most cases they point only to a rebuilding.

Some of the old forest farmhouses are very picturesque in appearance, and until comparatively recent years the whole of them were so. The same hand that bestowed upon them their interesting look was also the means of depriving them of it. Time endowed these old buildings with a charm, and time it was that rendered necessary their repair. Slate roofs and corrugated iron have now taken the place of thatch in many of them; walls have been rebuilt, and other changes effected, which, while conducing to convenience, have robbed them of much of their charm. At the same time there are those of them that remain much as they were far back in the centuries.

While all the ancient tenements are still occupied, many of the dwellings on the moor to which we have referred as being of later date are found in ruins, and a few have entirely disappeared. Of those of which only traces remain we may mention Hamlyn's House in Assacombe, Lambs' Down Farm above the valley of Dean Burn, Dolly's Cot on the hillside above Dartmeet, Petre's Pits House on Brent Moor, Brown's House on the hill above Wistman's Wood, and White's Slade on the East Dart. The latter is usually known as Snail's House from the tradition that attaches to it of two particularly buxom females who once lived there and subsisted on black slugs. I gathered the story many years ago from Mr. Richard Cleave, of Hexworthy, and subsequently I found a variant of it related on the South Teign, its locale there being a tinner's house below Metheral. That this should be so is not surprising, and is not the only instance we have on Dartmoor of similar stories being related of more than one place. We have already related the tradition of Fitz's Well on the Blackabrook, as well as its obvious variant attaching to the pool of the same name in Okehampton Park. Newhouse Inn, on the Princetown and Moreton road, has been spoken of as having been kept by the one time well-known Jan Roberts, whereas the little house of entertainment over which he presided was quite two miles distant. The story of Childe the Hunter may be a similar case, for while his tomb, or what tradition affirms to be such, exists in the forest, it also used to be pointed out at Tavistock. There is the instance of the story of Elfrida, which it has been sought to attach to that town, although it is quite clear that the tradition has no connection whatever with it, but belongs to Dorset. Events are easily transferred to places to which they do not belong; tradition speedily finds a home. The soul-land was placed by Homer beyond the ocean: Claudian brought it to the shores of Gaul, and later it was transferred to Britain.

Hen Tor House, above the west bank of the Plym, is another old homestall of which only the ruins are now to be seen. One of a later date is Fox Tor House, near the tor of that name, which was built by the despoiler of Childe's Tomb. In another part of the moor is Stat's House, and not far distant from this is Mandles, both solitary ruins. In their vicinity is Teign Head Farm, which has not been suffered to fall to decay. This, which is not a Forest Tenement, having been built late in the eighteenth century, is one of those that have received the attention of the modern builder, and lost much in appearance in consequence, for quite recently the old thatched roof has been replaced by one of slate. While this was in progress a certain lover of the moor happened to pass by, and learnt that the workmen had recently lost some four or five rounds of putty. Had this happened fifty years back suspicions that it had been spirited away might have been aroused, but as these did not present themselves the reason of the disappearance of the article in question had to be sought in another direction. But where had it gone? Naturally, it would be supposed that it could not go without hands. But it did. One of the farmer's sheepdogs was observed to be walking about very stiffly, and on examination it was found that he had the putty inside him.

The remains of a building exist on the right bank of the Dart not far below the clapper at Post Bridge. This is known as The Barracks, and once served as a dwelling-place for miners employed in the vicinity. All around Post Bridge the evidences of former mining operations are abundant, and it is near this place that the chief work of this character is now carried on. It is generally considered that King's Oven, which is about two miles distant, and which is mentioned in the Forest Perambulation of 1240, was once a place where ore was smelted. It may, however, be well to explain that no traces of a smelting-house now exists at King's Oven, and also that it has been suggested that the word 'oven' may be a corruption of the Saxon 'hof', a dwelling. Tradition tells us that the twelve knights who perambulated the forest when the latter was given by Henry III to his brother Richard rested here during the first night of their journey, which seems to show that it was something more than a place for smelting tin. But there was once another oven on Dartmoor that figured in traditions. It was situated at Longbetor, on the Wapsworthy Brook, and belonged to a certain shadowy 'old squire', who spent his time in hunting. He kept his own pack of hounds, and seemed to enjoy a run at lightning speed on those parts of the forest that nobody else could ride over. Another famous hunter was Tom French, but the hounds he hunted were a very irregular pack. But he accomplished the end he had in view, which was the destruction of foxes round Widecombe, where they had become so numerous as to cause considerable loss to farmers and villagers. When Tom's work in this direction was finished he still continued to follow hounds, but only for the enjoyment of hunting. Tom loved Dartmoor, and was known to everybody upon it between Widecombe and the Plym. The old settlement of Ponsworthy is in Tom French's country. This little place lies snugly in a valley, past which runs the West Webburn. A stone at the end of the parapet of the bridge that spans this stream bears the date 1666, but the name of the hamlet tells us that men dwelt here back in Saxon times.

Many years ago there lived in this secluded place an old labourer with his wife and little grandson, the latter having lost both his parents in infancy. When the boy was about eight years of age the old man died, leaving nothing to his widow but his scantily-furnished cottage, and to his grandson good advice. He had called the latter to his bedside a short time before he passed away and counselled him to be industrious and honest, to be faithful to his master when he should have one, and, above all, 'to mind his P's and Q's'. Little Noah promised to remember his grandfather's words, and the old man breathed his last peacefully.

For a few years Mary Hodge had a hard struggle, but as soon as Noah grew old enough to work the prospect brightened. Time passed on, and Noah began to earn regular wages. They were small enough in all conscience, but so were the wants of the two. Noah grew up to be a

Ponsworthy, on the West Webburn.

man, and was proud to feel that he was able to support his grandmother, now a very aged and almost helpless woman. He never forgot what his grandfather had told him, and felt thankful to him for giving him advice that he had found to be so valuable.

But days of trial were to come; a dark shadow was to rest upon that little cottage. Noah fell sick, and was confined to his room for many weeks. The sum he had contrived to save out of his wages became exhausted, and when he was at length able to come downstairs, though still far too weak to work, he found himself penniless. The neighbours helped him as well as they could, but they were themselves very poor, and how he was to live till he could again go to work he knew not. For himself he cared little; it was his old grandmother that filled his thoughts. Not only was she now entirely deprived of the few comforts he had hitherto been able to give her, but was almost in want of necessaries.

One morning as Noah sat by the hearth preparing some pea soup there was a knock at the door.

"Come in," he cried.

A gentleman entered.

"How far is it to Widecombe?" he asked.

"About two miles and a half, sir," replied Noah, rising. "Go straight up the road; you can't miss it."

"What kind of a place is it? You call it a town, don't you?"

Noah smiled.

"We do," he said; "but 'tis hardly the sort of town you've got in your mind, sir. But won't you please to take a seat?"

"Won't stop, thank you. Have to trudge to Widecombe, and from there to Moreton. Mustn't loiter by the way."

He was about to withdraw when he happened to notice the tall clock in the corner of the apartment.

"A fine clock," he said. "Want to sell it?"

"Couldn't do that, sir," answered Noah.

"I'm fond of old-fashioned things," explained the stranger. "I'll give you a good price for it."

The offer of money was tempting, and Noah hesitated. But it was only for an instant. The clock had been his grandfather's, and he would not have parted with it for ten times its value.

"I'm very sorry, sir," he said, "but that clock belonged –."

"I know, I know," interrupted the stranger. "Say no more. An old possession, eh? Well, I honour that feeling. Wouldn't take it from you for the world. Straight up the road eh, for Widecombe. Thanks, very much. Good morning."

"I wish you good morning, sir," said Noah.

The stranger departed, and Noah took up the spoon with which he had been stirring the soup before the vistor's arrival.

"I was glad to heer 'e spaik proper," observed his grandmother, who was seated in an armchair near the window. " 'Tis always right to do that. As poor dear Laban told 'e, always mind your P's and Q's."

Noah was about to attend once more to the preparation of the soup, when he suddenly turned away from the hearth and flung the spoon upon the table.

"Never mind the peas," he cried. "Let they take care o' themselves for once. It's the Q's I'm thinking about."

He passed hastily from the room, and presently returned with two small plates of iron. They were the shoes with which oxen were formerly shod, when those animals were employed in farm work, and from their shape were known as Q's.

"I'll be back in a minute or two, Granny," he said. "Perhaps the gentleman may fancy these. He's fond of old-fashioned things."

He left the cottage and hurried after his visitor.

Half-way up the hill his foot struck some small object lying in the road. It was a heavy purse. Then Noah went on faster than before, and soon coming in sight of the gentleman, called upon him to stop.

"Have you lost anything, sir?" he asked breathlessly, as he reached him.

The stranger searched his pockets.

"By Jove! Yes!" he cried. "I've lost my purse!"

"Here it be, sir," said Noah, handing it to him. "Glad I picked it up."

"Did I drop it in your house?"

"No, I found it in the road," replied Noah.

"Were you coming after me?"

"I was coming to ask you whether you cared for these, sir," replied Noah, holding forth the iron plates. " 'Tis what oxen used to be shoe'd wi' yeers agone, and I thought you might like to have mun. They'm purty old-fashioned, I b'lieve. Us call mun Q's."

"I will buy them of you," said the stranger, "if you will let me have them at my own price."

"You are welcome to them, if you wish," returned Noah.

"My own price," repeated the stranger. "I think you deserve this for them."

He put them in his pocket, and taking two sovereigns from his purse placed them in Noah's hand.

Noah got back to the cottage in good time to mind his peas, but was more particularly gratified that he had minded his Q's. They had proved the means of banishing the grim spectre of poverty. Once more his old grandmother had the little comforts he desired for her; the light of hope streamed into the cottage, and Noah's returning strength soon caused that hope to grow into a reality.

There are the usual traditions on Dartmoor of underground passages and secret ways. One of these is said to lead from Gidleigh Castle to the Teign, and another is near Shilston in the parish of Drewsteignton. The existence of some mining remains near Gidleigh Bridge probably gave rise to the belief in the former, while an adit that once drained Bradmere Pool seems to have been the foundation on which the latter was built. There is also the story of the manor lost at the card-table; of the feud between two parishes; and of concealments and escapes of Cavaliers or Roundheads during the Civil War; and many others that have their counterpart in various parts of England.

Dartmoor has had its poets. The best known of these is Carrington, who lies in the graveyard of Combehay, near Bath, but the one who has endeared himself to the moor people is Jonas Coaker, whose grave may be seen at Widecombe. Jonas was one of them; he spent the whole of his life in the land of tors, and was well versed in its lore.

I have said that traditions soon attach themselves to objects, and it may be that in some future day one will arise on the Wella Brook, the stream that runs down by the hill of Huntingdon to fall into the Avon. Here, on the left bank, a small enclosure may be seen, and within it, at one end, an upright stone with an incised cross, and in the centre two others, the lower one of these bearing the inscription *Deo Gloria*. The letters are quite fresh now, but when the storms of a few winters shall have beaten upon them, their age will not be apparent. Then, perhaps, a story will be attached to the little monument. Possibly the good brothers of the abbey of Buckfast, which is but a few miles off, will figure in this.

15

Ancient Customs

An old-world region such as Dartmoor is naturally the home of many curious customs. Some of these are similar to those found in most of our rural districts, while others are peculiar to itself. Not the least interesting are the customs formerly pertaining to the forest and the venville commons, of which traces now remain. These throw much light upon the history of the moor, as also do the customs of the tinners, who held their parliament on Crockern Tor during several centuries. Customs connected with the border manors, with the villages, and home life, and amusements of the people, have also an interest, particularly when it is possible to dicover their meaning. As we are not the fortunate possessors of the magic carpet of which we read in the *Arabian Nights*, we are unable to transport ourselves thither at our pleasure, but we can certainly go there in imagination. This we will do, and try to see something of the old usages that once obtained in that wild land.

When Dartmoor was bestowed upon Richard, Earl of Cornwall, by his brother Henry III, it lost its status as a royal forest, and became in law a chase. True forest courts could no longer be held, but courts of the chase and manor continued to assemble at Lydford, and the old customs connected with those matters over which the former had jurisdiction, still remained. We have already referred to the thirty-five ancient tenements in the forest, held by copy of Court Roll. On the Earl of Cornwall being created Duke, in 1336, this court became the Duchy Court and the holders of the tenements continue to attend it. Formerly it was held at Lydford, but early in the nineteenth century was removed to Princetown.

A custom formerly existed according to which a successor to an ancient tenement had the right of enclosing eight acres of clear ground, this being known as the newtake. Application had to be made to the steward of the manor of Lydford, who gave direction to the reeve of the forest, together with three owners of tenements, to view and measure the ground. Upon their certifying that this had been done the steward would make the applicant a grant of the land at the Duchy Court, three half-pence per acre being claimed for entering it on the Roll, and a rent of twelve pence yearly put upon it. The persons constituting the court were, and still are, sworn upon a reed, which, as has been remarked, is somewhat strange when we consider that the district in which this custom was observed is one not favourable to the growth of cereals. There is, however, abundant evidence that rye was formerly grown on the moor, and it is not unlikely that it was chiefly this kind of grain that found its way to the mill that we have already spoken of as existing in the forest at an early period.

On the verge of the commons surrounding the forest are certain properties lying in what is known as Venville. These vills sometimes consist of an entire parish, and sometimes of a group of a few farms, or even of a single farm. The owners possess rights of pasturage and turbary on the forest, and are also entitled to take stone and rushes for building and thatching. But they could only do this formerly by observing the 'custom of the forest'. His cattle were to "come to the Kyngs Forrest by Sonne and goo home by Sonne"; they were not permitted to remain there during the night, lest those in charge of them should interfere with the deer, a provision strictly in accordance with forest law. But when Dartmoor ceased to be a royal hunting ground this restriction was removed, and a fine, or rent, of a few pence yearly, was imposed upon the venville tenants, as the owners of the vills were termed, for night-rest, and this is still payable. Another 'custom of the forest' limited the pasturing of cattle by the venville men to such a number as they were able to winter upon their holdings; if they required to pasture more than that number, they were required to pay for them according to a certain scale. These rights still exist, as also does the prohibition to take "green oak and red venison". As very little of the former, and less of the latter, is to be seen on Dartmoor, the venville tenant may be said to have a right to take anything he can find there.

At the drifts, or periodical driving of the moor for the purpose of ascertaining whether any cattle are unlawfully pastured upon it, the venville men were formerly compelled to assist. On the day fixed for this, it was the custom for the priours, or those in whose charge the cattle were placed, to summon the venville men by blowing horns on the tors, very early in the morning. The horns were blown against a concave stone, by which means the volume of sound was increased.

One of these stones is to be seen in Quarry Lane, near Whitchurch Down. But the venville tenant was not suffered to go without a reward for his day's labour. This took the form of refreshment on arriving at Dunnabridge Pound, the enclosure to which all estrays were, and still are, driven, and consisted of a half-penny cake, 'according to the custom of the forest!'

As there can be no trespass in a forest, which is open ground, it might perhaps be thought that nothing could be claimed from the owners of cattle impounded there. But the Dartmoor man is resourceful. As a fine could not be imposed, he hit upon the expedient of making a charge for watering the cattle, and so proved himself a believer in the adage that there are more ways than one of cooking a potato.

Another old custom was that which enabled a 'squatter' to obtain land on which to erect a dwelling on delightfully easy terms. According to this, if a house could be erected, and a small piece of land enclosed, between sunrise and sunset they become the property of the builder. Preparations had to be kept secret; only those known to be willing to assist were made acquainted with what was intended to be done. Then, on the day fixed, the little party of builders and thatchers would meet, and immediately the sun rose operations would begin. The materials had been brought to the spot in readiness, and as the work proceeded briskly, it was usually well advanced before anybody discovered what was being done. The last of the houses on the moor to be built in accordance with this custom was that known as Jolly Lane Cot, about mid-way between the Forest Inn and the Dart at Hexworthy. My old friend, Mr. Richard Cleave, of the former, told me many years ago that he remembered the building of the house, and how that a fire burned upon the hearth before the setting of the sun. This practice of squatting could only have been carried out on sufferance; there does not appear to be any law of the forest that permitted it. It was prohibited by the Duchy on the erection of Jolly Lane Cot.

Several stories are told on the moor to account for the erratic manner in which some of the boundary lines between the commons surrounding the forest are set out. These state that the line when running in a manner other than it would be supposed to do was so carried in order to include a piece of the adjoining common which had been claimed under these circumstances. A corpse had been found there but had been refused burial by the commoners. Those to whom the other common belonged had gone over the boundary, and removing the body, had caused the necessary rites to be performed. They then claimed the piece of land on which they had entered, and fixed the bounds accordingly. An old document sets forth that if a man died by misfortune, or was slain, in the forest, "the crowner of Lydeford shall crowne and sytte vpon hym".

Early rising is healthful, and probably the tinners of Dartmoor found it so. But whether they did or not it is certain that they sometimes found it necessary. I have in my possession the copy of a precept issued in Queen Anne's time, directing that twenty-four jurats were to attend a court of the tinners to be held on Crockern Tor, and they were to assemble there at eight o'clock in the morning. A journey to the centre of the moor on a cold morning, there to sit on a block of granite till the business of the day was concluded, does not seem particularly inviting. But we suppose the tinners did not mind it. Undoubtedly they were men of mettle.

The laws passed at the Stannary Parliament were very stringent, and though the tinners themselves enjoyed many privileges, it would appear that they were also liable to many penalties. According to a tradition, a fearful punishment awaited that unhappy tinner who had been proved to be guilty of adulterating his tin. Three spoonfuls of the molten metal were poured down his throat! It was the custom of the tinners to use tools of oak, as is shown by the discovery in old workings of spades and picks of that wood. The discovery of flint implements in the hut circles of Dartmoor has been held to be a proof that they were not connected with the tin-mines, because, it has been said, men who were searching for tin ore would use implements of metal and not of stone. The discovery of wooden tools in the workings shows what this argument is worth.

Carew, the historian of Cornwall, tells us that it was customary for the tinners of that county to set fire to the roof of their blowing-houses, that is, the small houses in which the tin was smelted, after they had been standing some time, in order to obtain the grains of tin that had lodged in the thatch. It is not recorded whether the Dartmoor tinners – or 'old men', as they are always termed – followed this practice, but it is not improbable. The ruins of such erections are to be found in many of the valleys of the moor.

Some of the customs observed at the viewing of the bounds of the commons forming the purlieus of the forest are interesting, and may possibly be relics of ancient usages. It has been supposed that boundaries were once confided to the care of certain heathen deities, and that mysterious rites were performed at the stones marking them. The Phalaeni sacrificed themselves in order to extend the frontier of

Carthage, and were buried on the boundary line, where altars, or sepulchres, to their memory were afterwards erected. It is possible that some of the boundaries on Dartmoor, which were probably much the same in Saxon times as they are at the present day, were in existence before the coming of that people, and that at some of the stones by which they were marked similar sacrifices may have been made. But whether the bound-viewing customs on Dartmoor be relics of these, or have a later and different origin, they are none the less curious.

In viewing the bounds of a common it is customary on reaching a stream to force some of the party into it, and this is generally regarded as a mere humorous custom, though probably not by the victims. Others give the practice another meaning, and regard it as being intended to cause the members of the party to recollect the spot where the stream was crossed, and so preserve a memory of the boundary. But it is well to remember that in primitive times such dippings were also performed, and were regarded as necessary in order to wash evil influences out of that particular area that was being perambulated. Sometimes the ceremony is no more than the mere throwing of stones in the water at the points where the boundary touched the stream, and it may be that the one is simply a substitute for the other. There is again the custom of inflicting a blow upon some of the boys accompanying the bound-viewers on reaching a certain stone, and this is regarded as being intended to serve the same purpose as forcing people into the rivers, or enticing them to venture upon mires by the showering of nuts and fruit there, that is to say, to cause them to remember the spot. But this, too, appears to be a relic of a primitive custom. The boys were once regarded as representatives of human victims who had been sacrificed there, and the blow was given in order to cause them to shed tears, these being considered to act as a charm to bring rain to fertilise the earth. If the rainfall depended upon the tears shed at bound-viewings at the present day it is to be feared that Dartmoor would not long merit its title of a Land of Streams.

In some instances we find compensation made to those who suffer or run any risk at these ceremonies. When the bounds of Gidleigh Common are perambulated it is the custom for one of the boys of the party to climb the tall menhir under Kes Tor and stand upon the top of it, for which feat he is rewarded with the sum of sixpence. But as a matter of fact all who choose to attend on these occasions are remembered, for it is an invariable custom that ample refreshment shall be served to the party at a certain point on the boundary line.

Sometimes the spot derives its name from this, as in the case of Buckfastleigh Moor, where the point at which this pleasing function takes place is calling Sitting-down End.

The day set aside for viewing the bounds, which in a number of cases is done at regular periods, in a few instances bears a name. Thus at Okehampton the occasion is known as Spurling Day; at Bovey Tracey it is called Mayor's Monday, from the practice once observed by the portreeve of riding round a stone cross, which formed a boundary mark, on the day of his election, the first Monday after the 3rd of May. An important part of the ceremony was the striking of the stone with a stick. It is certain that when this was done it could not be said that the bounds had not been 'beaten'. This seems to be a very ancient custom, the cross, in all probability, having taken the place of the stone which was set up in prehistoric times on the site of an intended settlement. At the perambulation of Erme Plains, in southern Dartmoor, it was customary to read a proclamation at certain points setting forth the bounds of the manor of Ermington, and also the rights that were claimed by its lord. A net was also cast into the Erme and drawn for the purpose of maintaining the rights of fishery in that river.

On Dartmoor, as elsewhere, natural objects often form boundaries; in fact, the forest line is marked mostly by such. But the lines between the surrounding commons are in nearly every case defined by bond-stones. In a few instances a cross is found as a bondmark, but in such cases it is probable that these took the places of other stones. There is good evidence that one of these, now on the forest line, was standing in the Confessor's time, and marked the limits of land then held under grant from the king by Siward, Earl of Northumberland. On the other hand the four crosses that at one time marked the bounds of Brent Moor, of which only one now remains erect and in a complete state, would appear to be of later date. The marks set up by the tinners are mostly of two kinds. In some instances we find that these consist of small mounds, which the moormen call stannaburrows; in others the tin-bounds are marked by a few loose stones set up in the form of a brandis, that is the triangular stand placed on the hearth for setting the kettle on.

Among the customs observed at manor courts that which was at one time usual at Dunstone, in the parish of Widecombe, was probably of great antiquity. The court was held in the open air, and the chief rents were deposited by the tenants in a hollow in a large stone, which may still be seen. Attached to the manor of Walkhampton was the duty of

Holne Church.

124

providing accommodation for the king and his retinue for one night should he chance to pass that way. This was probably imposed at the time when the moor formed a royal hunting ground.

Perhaps the most interesting among the customs observed in the Dartmoor country is that known as the Holne Ram Feast, or Ram Roasting. That this was the relic of an ancient ceremony, the meaning of which was forgotten by those who took part in it, there can be little doubt. It was customary in former times for the youths of the neighbourhood to assemble in the Play Field before sunrise on May Day, and then make their way to the moor. A ram lamb was then caught and brought to the field. It was then secured to a menhir that stood there, and slaughtered, after which it was roasted whole. At mid-day it was cut up, and all present made it their business to obtain a portion of it, as the eating of it was supposed to bring good luck during the ensuing year. Latterly the ram was secured beforehand; the people assembled later and various sports took place, the day being regarded merely as a local holiday. But that these proceedings were the distortion of rites once held to be important can hardly be doubted. In early times the ram was probably offered as a sacrifice.

The village of Holne is delightfully situated on the verge of the moor. Near the church is the ancient Church House Inn, of which some hundred and forty years ago Edward Collins, who seems to have been a true type of the Dartmoor border man, was the landlord. He lies in the quiet churchyard, on the side of the hill that sweeps down to the chase he knew so well.

In some of the border villages the stocks in which it was customary to confine offenders may still be seen, and at Belstone are the two pillars that formerly supported the bar to which the long beam of the ducking-stool, or ducking chair, was suspended. Another old-time punishment was that of 'riding the stang' or 'skimmeting', which consisted of a burlesque procession, in which men, dressed in imitation of those persons whom it was intended to ridicule, mounted on a horse, or donkey, 'rode to water'. Here the victims were supposed to be ducked, but those who represented them naturally not desiring this part of the ceremony to be too realistic, usually omitted it and in its place generally set about sprinkling the spectators.

It is not so long since the Sunday revel was to be seen in the villages bordering Dartmoor, but that this custom has disappeared nobody will lament. The ancient fairs still continue, though not exactly in the form known to our fathers. The well-known Widecombe Fair is held; and at

Tavistock Jan's Fair and Joan's Fair, the latter being usually known as Goose Fair, still take place. Brent Fair continues to attract large numbers, and so do others in the moorland district. Princetown Fair has taken the place of the one formerly held at Two Bridges. The Giglet at Okehampton is not now as it once was. Perhaps it is hardly necessary to state this when it is remembered that this was a wife market. It was held on the Saturday after Christmas, and its chief feature was the exercising of the privilege conferred on the young men of the neighbourhood, who were allowed to introduce themselves to any damsel that might take their fancy 'with a view to matrimony'.

At these fairs old convivial customs still obtain. When men drink together from the same mug, the latter must always 'go round the sun', that is to say, it must be passed from right to left, as cards are dealt. If anyone present happens to sneeze he must pay for an extra pint of ale.

It was once customary at burials at Manaton to carry the coffin three times round a cross in the churchyard before taking it into the church. Very probably the origin of the custom was unknown to those who latterly observed it. For this we must look back to primitive times, and then we shall find that it was a survival of a ceremony that once possessed a deep meaning. A belief existed that the nearer to the cross a corpse was interred the sooner would the soul be released from purgatory. It would not at all times be possible to form the grave very near to the sacred object, but the body could be taken to it, and probably it was hoped that this would have the same effect. Another custom connected with burials is that of resting the coffin on the side of Dartmeet Hill when being taken from the forest to Widecombe. The rock on which it is set down is known as the Coffin Stone.

❊❊❊❊❊

16

The Tree

The word forest is usually associated in our minds with trees, but its true signification was a royal hunting ground, defined by certain metes and bounds, and subject to laws of its own. It was not necessarily a tree-covered tract; all that was required was sufficient cover for the deer. This would be found on Dartmoor, although it is certain that trees never grew there to any extent. There is evidence that such were once to be seen in some of its more sheltered combes; indeed, in a few places a grove of dwarf oaks yet exists, while on the borders of the waste there were extensive woods as at the present time.

To these ancient groves, the remains of the scanty sylvan honours that Dartmoor may once have boasted, historical or traditionary associations attach in a few instances. But while these groves chiefly consist of oaks, the tree which is connected with Druidism, no story of that priesthood has come down to us. It has been remarked that throughout Devon no legend concerning the Druids exists, and by some this has been held to show that they were never known here. But the prehistoric people of the moor must have had some religion, and since Cæsar tells us that Druidism flourished in our island, it would be unsafe to say that it was unknown on Dartmoor. To find traces of Druidic worship in every stone monument, as the earlier antiquaries imagined they did, would be impossible now that their real meaning is more clearly recognised; but it could not be maintained that Druids never were on Dartmoor, for the reason that we can no longer connect them with those remains. While we may be unable to share the views of the antiquaries of a former day, we should refrain from going to the opposite extreme, and denying the existence of the ancient priesthood here entirely.

But not only are there no legends connected with the Druids and the oak groves of Dartmoor, but very few traditions concerning trees of any kind. Perhaps this is to be explained by the fact that they were always scarce there. In the folklore of many countries the tree figures prominently. In primitive times a man was not only commemorated by the setting up of a stone, but often a tree was also planted close by. On Dartmoor, as we have seen, numerous examples of the menhir, or memorial stone, exists, but in no instance is there a tree near by. Whether any were ever planted, there is nothing to show, but we can well understand how, if such were the case, they would hardly be likely to flourish, and that we should see nothing of them today. But one or two moorland traditions do tell us of the planting of some trees. It is said that Wistman's Wood, on the West Dart, was planted by Isabella de Fortibus, Countess of Devon, but it is clear to the most casual observer that the story is without any foundation. The monks of Buckland, who once owned a tract on Dartmoor extending from the Walkham to the Plym, are said to have been the first to plant the apple tree in the valley of the Tavy, which has been long renowned for the excellence of its orchards. This may have been the case, and yet it would not be wise to accept the statement on the evidence of tradition alone. An expression, earlier indeed than the time of the abbey of Buckland, may have been responsible for it. It is possible that the monks were said by those who recognised their usefulness to have "planted a wood of fruit-bearing trees", by which they meant, as ancient writers had done with regard to other places, that they had sown the good seed of faith and that a harvest was to be looked for.

The ancient ceremony of wassailing the apple trees on Christmas Eve, though once observed in the farmhouses in the parishes surrounding Dartmoor, could never have formed one of the customs of those actually dwelling upon it, seeing that apples did not grow there. Of orchards there were none, but we do remember the pride with which a certain old Dartmoor cotter regarded the two or three apple trees that grew in her little garden. We refer to Mrs. Satterly – Sally Satterly, as she was called by her acquaintances – of Jolly Lane Cot, which we have referred to as having been erected in accordance to a custom that once obtained on the moor.

In the northern mythology it was believed that the first man was created out of the sacred ash, which was named Yggdrasil, and the Saxon is said to have regarded that tree with a mysterious feeling. He planted it by his dwelling, and near some of the more ancient Dartmoor farmsteads we still find it flourishing, together with the sycamore. The custom of burning the ashen faggot on Christmas Eve is still observed in some farmhouses, but it is not often that it is carried out in its entirety. Once it was usual to place a boy on the faggot for a brief space. This was supposed to be for the purpose of testing his courage, but it was probably a relic of that heathen rite which is described as the passing of children through the fire to Moloch.

The graceful mountain ash, or, as it is called on Dartmoor, the quickbeam, is not infrequently met with in sheltered hollows, or in the narrow valleys. Several are to be seen at Hangman's Pit, the hollow on Holne Moor to which we have already referred, and near by are the ruins of huts and other remains. Among these, on Horn Hill, are two fallen menhirs and a triple stone row.

The tree appears in a few of the place-names of Dartmoor, and this may point to its former existence at those spots or, in one or two instances at all events, be merely a corruption of an older name, the meaning of which is forgotten. A part of Cut Combe, one of the most solitary spots in the northern quarter of the forest, is known to the moormen as Fur Tor Wood, but no trees are to be seen there now. Yet it is not improbable that the name really does owe its origin to the former presence here of trees, that is to say of a few dwarf oaks. The combe is sheltered, and there seems no reason why they should not grow here as well as in the valleys of the Dart or Erme. Not very far from it a friend of mine once found a piece of oak, partly buried in the peat. The disappearance of trees in similar spots on the moor is probably in some instances to be attributed to the tinners, who may have desired to supplement their supply of peat fuel with good oak logs. Of course the felling of these trees would be contrary to the law of the forest at one time, but when the latter was no more used as a hunting ground, and the deer became scarce, it is not unlikely that this law was little regarded.

Hazel Tor, or, as it is now usually called, Ausewell Rock, probably did derive its name from the hazel, since it is placed on a hill that is still covered in places with trees and undergrowth; but, judging from an early form of the name, we cannot suppose with probability that Aish in Widecombe and in Brent owed their names to the ash. Quickbeam Hill, on the Erme, we may very well imagine owes its name to the tree so-called; but it is certain that The Ockery, Water Oke Corner, and other similar names have nothing whatever to do with the oak, but were derived from the Celtic 'ock', meaning 'water'.

The best known of the oak groves of Dartmoor is Wistman's Wood above Two Bridges. But there are others that the rambler will come upon. In the romantic gorge through which the West Ockment pursues its way from the forest is one which is full of interest. It is usually spoken of by the moormen as Blackater, i.e., Black Tor Copse, but is referred to in a document of the 29th of Elizabeth as Blacketers Beare. On the beautiful Erme is another, which is known as Piles Wood, and this is shown on an old map which appears to be of sixteenth century date. At Brimpts, on the East Dart, is another grove, while in the gorge lower down that stream as well as in Huccaby Cleave, which is also near by, dwarf oaks still grow in some luxuriance.

Among the more celebrated oak trees in the Dartmoor country may be mentioned the Meavy Oak, under the spreading boughs of which it is probable that in old time the villagers often gathered, as the pupils and patients of Hippocrates gathered beneath the boughs of the plane tree of Cos, to hear the delivery of that in which they were concerned. On the bank of the Tavy at Tavistock once stood the famous Lady Howard's Oak, regarded in former days with a feeling almost amounting to awe, from its connection with the mysterious mistress of Fitzford. Another that has gone down before the hand of time is the Fatal Oak of Tamerton, under which the godson of John Copleston of Warleigh fell dead, pierced by the dagger which the latter cast at him in anger. At Piles is the Crooked Oak, well known to the hunter of southern Dartmoor; and near Wo Brook Foot the Mill Oak, a tree which grows within the ruined walls of an ancient blowing-house.

In other of the border villages where fine trees are to be seen may be named South Tawton, North Bovey, Manaton, Sampford Spiney, Peter Tavy, and Mary Tavy.

A tradition tells us that an avenue of trees once extended from Forstall Cross towards Lydford; and another that the beeches in the vicarage lawn at Brent were planted by men who brought them to the spot when saplings in the manner that children bestride a stick in imitation of riding a horse. In the hedgerows on the borders of the moor the hazel is found in plenty, the bush from which is cut the magic wand that tells of the presence of water; and in the cottage gardens everywhere grows the elder, or, as it is sometimes called, the Judas Tree, from the tradition that it was on one of this kind that the betrayer hanged himself. At Moreton until a few years ago stood the pollard elm, renowned as the Punch Bowl, or the Dancing Tree, deriving the first name from the form into which its branches had been trained, and the latter from the use to which it was formerly put, it being customary at certain times to lay a platform in the hollow that represented the bowl and for dances to take place there. For some years before its fall only a portion of its trunk remained, but it put forth its leaves nevertheless, like the ancient tree that grew amid the ruins of Babylon, which time had similarly dealt with, and which the Arabs believed had survived the desolation of the ancient city. Though Dartmoor and its borderland may be unable to boast of so wonderful a tree as that described in the *Similitudes of Hermas*, it will yet be admitted, I think that there are not wanting some to which interest attaches.

Sam Gaskett lived at Meavy, and worked as a miner in the neighbourhood. But such employment was precarious, and even when there was a demand for labour the money to be earned was very little. Wages depended upon the yield of tin, and as this was not to be found in great quantity it was seldom that more than would suffice for the bare necessaries of living was carried home on the Saturday night. But Sam kept a good heart. He was brave in spite of his poverty, and felt confident that things would be better by-and-by. In this view of his circumstances he was seconded by his wife, who declared that a time would come when there must be a change, since it was a long lane that had no turning.

It was a winter night, and Sam sat on a low stool looking into the peat fire and wondering when the time would arrive that would see him better off. His wife, seated on a chair on the other side of the hearth, was busily employed in knitting, stopping now and again to assure herself that the babe in the cradle in front of her was sleeping peacefully.

"They old men have a clained out the workin's purty well," said Sam, after a time. "They ant lef much tin for us. I'm feared I shall have to shift if it daun't get better soon Mary. But where to go to? That's what I can't tell."

"It may not always be like this Sam," returned Mary. "You said so yourself only yesterday."

"I did, I'll awn. But as the days go by, and nothin' com's along, a man's obliged to alter he's tune. I'm purty nigh down to my last penny. That's a poor look out, bant it? But there," Sam continued, " 'tidn' no good lookin' 'pon the black side of a thing. Say no more about it; us'll see how 'tis by-m-by."

He rose and lighted a lantern.

"Must get a bit more turve," he said. "I forgot to see to 't when I com' home."

There was no outhouse attached to the little cottage in which Sam lived, and for the want of this it had been his custom to stack his peat in the hollow trunk of the oak that stood on the green near the churchyard gate. Here his store of fuel was as well sheltered as though it were

The Meavy Oak.

beneath a roof, and as the cavity was large it was capable of containing all that he needed.

Sam walked across the green, holding his lantern before him for the night was intensely dark, and on reaching the tree, at once set about filling the basket he had brought with him. Some of the peat had fallen from the little stack, and while taking up this his hand encountered some small object that lay close to the trunk of the tree. Throwing the light from his lantern upon it he saw that it was a purse. It was covered with peat dust and seemed to have lain where he had found it for some time.

When he reached home he showed it to his wife.

"Us be all right now, Mary," he said. "What you've always said be com' to pass."

He opened the purse, and Mary saw that it contained three or four shining gold coins.

"Guineas!" cried Sam. "Us be rich now."

"We are no richer than before, Sam," said Mary. "The purse does not belong to us. You must try to find the owner of it."

"You'm right," replied Sam, closing the purse. "I was hopin' – but there, us'll say no more. I'll see 'bout it tomorrow."

Sam Gaskett kept his word, and made inquiries of everyone in the neighbourhood whether they had heard of anything having been lost, but was careful not to say exactly what it was. But he could learn nothing. It was certain that the purse belonged to nobody living in, or around, Meavy, and he could only come to the conclusion that it had been dropped where he found it by some passing traveller who had taken shelter within the hollow tree. But he and Mary agreed that the purse should not be touched, and it was put carefully by in a drawer of an old bureau that had once been the pride of his grandfather.

A week passed away, and then Sam came home one evening with some good news. The captain of the mine had offered him the position of overman, which meant higher and regular wages. But though Sam had gladly accepted this post, it was not without some doubt that he did so. He feared, so he told Mary, that he was "hardly skollard enough for the job".

Mary was equal to the occasion.

"You know your letters, Sam," she said, "and you can spell little words well enough. All you want is to learn to write. Do you know what you must do? You must go to school, Sam."

"Go to school?"

"To be sure. John Gregory will be glad to have you evenings after his boys be gone."

And so it was arranged. Sam went to school regularly, and was soon able to do all that was required of him as overman.

But his good fortune did not last, for before another winter came the mine had ceased working, and Sam found himself without employment. He had saved a little, and this enabled him to live for a few months, but the inevitable at length came. The middle of the winter found him penniless.

Then it came about that he once more sat and looked into the glowing peat and wondered whether he should ever rise from his poverty. He had still the same brave heart, but nevertheless his lip quivered as he looked at Mary and the little one in the cradle. He turned his glance away swiftly, and his eyes rested on the old bureau.

"Mary," he said, "I'm gwain' to aupen that puss."

She looked at him musingly for a few moments, and then her glance, too, fell on the child.

"Try once more to find the owner, Sam," she said. "If you cannot, than I think –"

There was a knock at the door, and Sam rose and opened it. The light from the peat fire revealed a rider, wearing a heavy travelling coat.

"Am I all right for Tavistock?" he asked.

"Up the road yonder," said Sam, indicating its direction. "Straight on for Dousland, an' there they'll shaw 'e the wan to take."

"You call this place Meavy, don't you?" asked the stranger.

"That's of it, sir."

"I thought so. I have not passed this way for some time, but I fancied I remembered it. It must be hereabout that I once lost my purse."

Mary heard the words, and came to the door.

"Lost your purse, did you, sir," exclaimed Sam. "Well, I found wan wance. If so be 'tis yours –"

"When did you find it?" inquired the stranger.

"Let me see," mused Sam; "when was it? Aw, I knaw; 'twas 'fore I went to school, sir."

"Before you went to school!" cried the stranger. "What on earth is the good of talking about that? Anyone who found a purse of mine then is welcome to it, and to all that it contains. Good-night."

He set off at a brisk trot, and was speedily lost to view in the darkness.

"There you be, Mary," said Sam, going to the old bureau and taking out the purse. " 'Tis mine now, right enough. 'Twasn' for nothin' I nailed the hoss-shoe auver the door when us com' heer. Some say there ban't nort in it. No; because they turn the points downwards, an' the luck rins out. Kaip the points like a man ought to kaip his heart and his head – up, to be sure. There's more in these old things than some people think for."

❋❋❋❋❋

❊❊❊❊❊

Two other titles available from the publishers by the same author :–

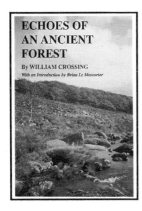

ECHOES OF AN ANCIENT FOREST
by William Crossing. Price £4.95
ISBN: 0 9515274 4 4 (Paperback)
Never previously published in book form, 'Echoes of an Ancient Forest' first appeared as a series of articles in *The Western Morning News* in 1901/02. Essentially, it is a history of Dartmoor interspersed with intriguing legendary stories, but as Brian Le Messurier states in the introduction it is more than that as Crossing's essays of the Perambulation, Isabella de Fortibus, the Reeves and the Foresters and so on are all written from the point of view of one who knows the places he is discussing.

THE LAND OF STREAM AND TOR
by William Crossing. Price £2.95
ISBN: 0 9515274 5 2 (Paperback)
Another work from this renowned Dartmoor author, which has hitherto been virtually unobtainable. It was originally a long article written for *Doidge's Western Counties Illustrated Annual* for 1892 and includes vivid descriptions of the vestiges of the habitations of the living and the sepulchral monuments of the dead, tin-mining and other historical notes on Dartmoor. Mention is also made of Wistman's Wood, Cranmere Pool, The Dewerstone and the Princetown area, and there are some fascinating accounts of the legendary Dartmoor Pixies.